# When God Turns Our Mourning into Joy

Elvetha Derrick-Telemaque

**TEACH Services, Inc.**
P U B L I S H I N G
www.TEACHServices.com • (800) 367-1844

World rights reserved. This book or any portion thereof may not be copied or reproduced in any form or manner whatever, except as provided by law, without the written permission of the publisher, except by a reviewer who may quote brief passages in a review.

The author assumes full responsibility for the accuracy of all facts and quotations as cited in this book. The opinions expressed in this book are the author's personal views and interpretations, and do not necessarily reflect those of the publisher.

This book is provided with the understanding that the publisher is not engaged in giving spiritual, legal, medical, or other professional advice. If authoritative advice is needed, the reader should seek the counsel of a competent professional.

Copyright © 2017 Elvetha Derrick-Telemaque

Copyright © 2017 TEACH Services, Inc.

ISBN-13: 978-1-4796-0796-9 (Paperback)

ISBN-13: 978-1-4796-0797-6 (ePub)

ISBN-13: 978-1-4796-0798-3 (Mobi)

Library of Congress Control Number: 2017910182

All scripture quotations, unless otherwise indicated, are taken from the King James Version (KJV). Public Domain.

Scripture quotations marked (NKJV) are taken from the New King James Version®. Copyright ©1982 by Thomas Nelson. Used by permission. All rights reserved.

Scripture quotations marked (NIV) are taken from the Holy Bible, New International Version®, NIV®. Copyright © 1973, 1978, 1984, 2011 by Biblica, Inc.® Used by permission. All rights reserved worldwide.

Scripture quotations marked (GNT) are from the Good News Translation in Today's English Version–Second Edition Copyright ©1992 by American Bible Society. Used by Permission.

**TEACH Services, Inc.**
PUBLISHING
www.TEACHServices.com • (800) 367-1844

# *Table of Contents*

**Introduction**......................................................5
**Chapter 1** Behold Him.............................................7
**Chapter 2** Rejoicing in His Presence.............................10
**Chapter 3** Keeping God's Purpose in Focus.......................14
**Chapter 4** Experiencing His Possibility.........................18
**Chapter 5** Experiencing His Intervention........................20
**Chapter 6** Faithfulness in Prayer Yields Rewards................22
**Chapter 7** Experiencing His Healing: The Great Exchange.........24
**Chapter 8** Releasing the Problem to Him.........................28
**Chapter 9** Experiencing His Power...............................31
**Chapter 10** Experiencing His Deliverance........................34
**Chapter 11** Submitting to His Transformation....................37
**Chapter 12** Basking in His Ability to Restore...................40
**Chapter 13** Pathways to God's Blessings.........................43
**Chapter 14** Experiencing God's Constancy........................47
**Chapter 15** Allowing God to Transform Your Trajectory: Connecting with His Promises.................50
**Chapter 16** Transformation Awaits You...........................54
**Chapter 17** Experiencing His Peace..............................71
**Chapter 18** Experiencing God's Faithfulness.....................96
**Chapter 19** Experiencing Confidence in God Against all Odds....117
**Chapter 20** Abiding in His Presence............................119
**Chapter 21** The Secret to Spiritual Wellness...................121
**Chapter 22** The Joy of Surrender...............................130
**Chapter 23** Finding Pleasure in Trusting.......................138
**Chapter 24** Allowing Him to Forgive Us.........................147
**Chapter 25** Experiencing His Restoration.......................155
**Chapter 26** Approaches For Focusing Your Prayer................172
**Chapter 27** One Week Prayer Retreat............................175

— important
— apply

# *Introduction*

# *Transforming The Trajectory of A Woman's Experience: The Power of Prayer*

Prayer is talking to God as to a friend—telling Him about our joys, sorrows, and concerns, or just talking to Him and listening for His response. I can still remember when I was young and tender, my grandfather invited me to kneel by the bedside to pray before going to sleep. He taught me the Lord's Prayer and the twenty-first psalm. We prayed those prayers every evening. Then one day, I asked my granddad, "Where in the heavens is God? Is He hearing our prayers?"

He replied, "Yes, God hears our prayers."

Then I said, "He sure has big ears because people everywhere are praying at the same time."

My granddad said, "He hears and answers everyone." I believed that God heard and answered my prayer. As I grew, I learned that prayer is talking to God as to a friend. If I am scared, I can tell Him, and He will protect me and keep me calm. If I am worried, He could reassure me. If

> *Prayer is talking to God as to a friend—telling Him about our joys, sorrows, and concerns, or just talking to Him and listening for His response.*

I lack confidence, He can remind me that He is able to help me and I can achieve my goals.

Many times we experience challenges, and the only One who understands and can help us is Jesus. The challenge is we cannot look into His eyes, yet we know that He is hearing and answering our prayers. We cry out to Him from deep in our souls, and we have the assurance that He hears and answers our prayers. When doubt creeps into our hearts, we just have to return to the last place where we were when He miraculously delivered us. Therefore, when we pray, we can pour out our petitions and leave that scared place with peace in our hearts, knowing that our petitions are heard.

In the Bible, there are many stories, promises, and experiences of answered prayers in the lives of men and women. This book will examine the transforming power of prayer in their lives and draw from these experiences to lead others to a dynamic prayer life. Join me as we examine the transformative power of prayer through the lens of God's faithfulness to His children.

The book takes us on a journey where we will explore the process of transformation through the lens of beholding, rejoicing in, and trusting God in every situation, the conditions that lead to prayer, how God responds to our prayers, and how we may continue to live a life of rejoicing in His presence. It is my hope that the words in this book will be like a downpour of rain in our souls that will lead us into a transformative prayer experience.

*Chapter 1*

# *Behold Him*

"In the year that king Uzziah died I saw also the Lord sitting upon a throne, high and lifted up, and his train filled the temple. Above it stood the seraphims: each one had six wings; with twain he covered his face, and with twain he covered his feet, and with twain he did fly. And one cried unto another, and said, 'Holy, holy, holy, is the Lord of hosts: the whole earth is full of his glory.' And the posts of the door moved at the voice of him that cried, and the house was filled with smoke. Then said I, 'Woe is me! for I am undone; because I am a man of unclean lips, and I dwell in the midst of a people of unclean lips: for mine eyes have seen the King, the Lord of hosts.' Then flew one of the seraphims unto me, having a live coal in his hand, which he had taken with the tongs from off the altar: And he laid it upon my mouth, and said, 'Lo, this hath touched thy lips; and thine iniquity is taken away, and thy sin purged.' Also I heard the voice of the Lord, saying, 'Whom shall I send, and who will go for us?' Then said I, 'Here am I; send me'" (Isaiah 6:1–8).

The most important element in transformation is beholding Jesus. In Him, we discover that change is possible. When I was a little girl, I copied the walking, writing, and speaking style of my favorite teacher. When I accepted Jesus, I experienced the purification that only comes from His blood. I purpose to copy His style every day of my life. My mind continues to look beyond my challenges to behold God. When I look to God, He turns my thoughts upward to see Him standing in His temple. His presence is so powerful and transformational that I could only exclaim, 'Holy! Holy! Holy! Lord God Almighty.' Even the angels proclaim His name and recognize His power to the extent that they cannot look at His visage, but must cover their faces. Holy awe filled their minds and thoughts; they are transformed by God's presence.

In the presence of Jesus, our hearts respond with singing, prayer, and testimony. The mind becomes exposed to who God is. We experience His power and majesty. We can no longer dwell in doubt, fear, or anxiety. We look upwards when challenges come. We look to Jesus in difficult times, and our hearts respond in singing, for in His presence is joy always. In every challenge, we go to Him in prayer and wait expectantly to hear Him speak to us. We sense His presence and power. Instead of complaining, we sing praises to God and tell others what He has done and is doing for us.

Testimony and praise lead us to experience a continual cleansing. Isaiah said in verses 6 and 7 that the angel flew down and touched his "lips with the burning coal and said, 'This has touched your lips, and now your guilt is gone, and your sins are forgiven'" (GNT). Beholding Jesus leads us to experience a new life in Christ. We are no longer guilty before God, but rather joyful and happy. His presence renews our hearts and minds, and His grace transforms us. He sets us free from our guilt and shame and liberates us from the fearful spirit that controls us. Bitterness, anger, passion, and a hostile spirit dissipates from our minds. When challenges come, we no longer shout insults and emanate hate. We display a quiet spirit filled with God's grace. A tender heart replaces the hateful stony heart, and we are ready to forgive others.

We forgive because we experienced God's transformational power and forgiveness. When we forgive, we benefit significantly. The act of forgiveness is for the wronged and the wrongdoer. Because we experienced forgiveness, we extend it to others. This act frees our minds and hearts to serve and praise God. It facilitates spiritual, emotional, mental, and physical healing (see Ephesians 4:17–32). The blood of Jesus purifies and cleanses us from all sins. All we need to do is ask, believe, and submit to His transforming blood and power.

The transformed soul partners with God to lead others into a relationship with Him. When Isaiah beheld God's power, grace, and love, he responded to God's call. He said, "I heard the voice of the Lord, saying,

'Whom shall I send, and who will go for us?' Then said I, 'Here am I; send me'" (Is. 6:8). The Great Commission becomes real and personal to the individual who has experienced forgiveness, mercy, and grace. The desire to share God's love and lead others to behold Him motivates us to say, "Come, see a man who told me all about myself" (see John 4:29)—a man who changed me from a fearful, doubting, anxious sinner to a confident saint. Behold the Lamb of God who is the only One to transform our hearts, minds, and souls. Look to Him, for in His presence is power, love, mercy, and grace. His blood is the only transforming force that helps us experience new life and desires. Lift up your eyes unto the Lord; your help comes from Him.

He is able to help and strengthen you in every situation. Lift up your eyes unto Him and behold His power. He can help you if you are sick, financially depressed, naked, fearful, or lost. Behold Him and keep your focus on Jesus. Your challenges will dissipate, and your life will be transformed.

Beholding Jesus is the prerequisite to experiencing transformation. His presence is so powerful that we yield to His love and molding. When God places His hands on our minds, hearts, and spirits, we relinquish hateful, angry, hostile, unforgiving, and anxious thoughts. We experience peace, joy, and love. We are overwhelmed with the desire to help others experience the same thing that we did. We say, "Come, see a man, who told me all that I have done and has touched my life. I am a new creation. I am a brand new individual." Jesus attracted my attention; I beheld Him, and now I am no longer the same. His grace and love transformed me.

> *Beholding Jesus is the prerequisite to experiencing transformation.*

---

*In my time of troubles I turn to Jesus to fully begin to experience the love and transformation that is about to occur. I am ready to experience this change that is coming.*

## Chapter 2
# *Rejoicing in His Presence*

Have you ever wanted to spend time with someone special? Were you excited when the time finally arrived? I remember when my fiancé was coming to my home to meet my family for the first time; I was excited; I could not contain myself. I hardly slept the night before. Then he arrived, flashing his radiant smile. Every moment was precious. Could you imagine what it is like spending time in the presence of Jesus? Knowing that He understands, loves, cares, and is working to transform your life? When I am in God's presence, I feel rested, safe, transformed, and relaxed. How about you?

In God's presence, there is a calm, resting feeling. We feel strengthened, joyful, and honored while we are in God's presence. In 1 Chronicles 16:27, we read, "Glory and honour are in his presence; strength and gladness are in his place" The reality of this text gives positive energy, gladness, and reasons to shout praises to the One who deserves the honor. We experience affirmation, respect, and honor in God's presence. The text tells us that majesty is found in God's presence. Do you know how majesty feels? Try to picture how members of the Royal Family feel—they feel special, relevent, blessed, honored, affirmed, and respected—in God's presence the woman of God experiences these positive emotions. We feel blessed, not arrogant; we feel honored, not demeaned; we feel affirmed, not downtrodden. His presence renews our strength, and we are honored to be in the presence of the Most High.

There is silence when an important person is speaking. The mind is empty of everything else, for everyone wants to hear what he/she is saying. Therefore, rejoicing in His presence suggests that we listen intently and push sadness, anxiety, fear, uncertainty, and negative emotions swiftly away; in fact, they evaporate and are replaced with joy, peace, confidence, hope, trust, and love. Rejoicing in His presence suggests that we keep our eyes fixed on Jesus. Keeping your eyes fixed on Jesus is a necessary prerequisite for rejoicing in His presence.

In God's presence, we are captivated by His awe, feel the urge to reverence Him, and surrender to His transforming power. Women of God, the transforming power of God's holy presence provides a glimpse of His Shekinah glory. As we gaze on His glory and sense His greatness and majesty, we surrender to His transforming power. In this metamorphic state, we turn away from self, release anxiety, and focus on His majestic beauty. In His presence, we experience complete joy and lasting peace. Mary knew what that meant when she responded to the angel: "Behold the maidservant of the Lord! Let it be to me according to your word" (Luke 1:38, NKJV). The psalmist David experienced this awesome power when he declared in Psalm 16:11, "You will show me the path of life; in your presence is the fullness of joy; at your right hand are pleasures forevermore" (NKJV). Just stop reading right now and reflect on being in God's presence, sitting at His right hand and experiencing the forever pleasures of being in love with Him. When my sons were two and four years old, the youngest always wanted to be on the right side. When he was there, he felt safe, special and loved. My older son, Shemaiah, would just smile and give him the right side. At times, he would say, "Mom what is on your right side that makes him feel special?" Kemuel would just ignore him while flashing his triumphant look.

In God's presence, there is triumph over sin, self, and evil. We are safe in His presence. His presence empowers us, and He transforms the trajectory of our experiences. We are changed from sadness to joy, hating to loving, and anxiety to peace. He has the power to sprinkle fresh, clean water—the refreshing of His holy presence—on us to cleanse us and renew our minds (see Ezekiel 36:26). Then, He will replace our negative spirit with His obedient spirit so that we may walk in His presence forever. In this transformed mind, we will prosper and never experience famine and poverty. We will prosper in His presence. Our children will be blessed, our storehouses will be filled, and our dreams will be fulfilled. In Psalm 16:11, David espoused that "You will show me the path of life; in your presence is the fullness of joy; at your right hand are pleasures forevermore" (NKJV). The result is the inflow of His grace and mercy, the outflow of His love to others, and the overflow of His mercy, love, and forgiveness to those around us (see Exodus 33:14).

Woman of God, when conviction perfumes our hearts and minds, the righteousness of God's presence illumines our souls and we long to be renewed, restored to communion with God, and connected with His Spirit. Daily, we submit to His leading and yearn to be in His presence (White, *Steps to Christ*, p 24).

In God's presence, we sense our sinful state and behold God's spotless character. We long to be like Jesus. We bow in penitence before His awesomeness and submit our desires, plans, and lives to Him. In His presence, we experience transformation. In this transformed state, we lose selfishness, unholy thoughts, and arrogance. The Holy Spirit takes hold of us, and we surrender to His leading that we may continue to grow in grace.

When the prophet Daniel beheld the glory surrounding the heavenly messenger that was sent unto him, he was overwhelmed with a sense of his weakness and imperfection. Describing the effect of the magnificent scene, he says, "There remained no strength in me: for my comeliness was turned in me into corruption, and I retained no strength" (Daniel 10:8). "The soul thus touched will hate its selfishness, abhor its self-love, and will seek, through Christ's righteousness, for the purity of heart that is in harmony with the law of God and the character of Christ" (White, *Step to Christ*, p. 29).

Thus, in His presence, we rejoice in rough times, challenging times, the storm, under persecution, and harsh treatment; there is joy in every situation. This joy comes from yielding to God, allowing His presence to flow into our minds and hearts, and overflow to those around us.

We praise in His presence. "And Mary said, My soul doth magnify the Lord, and my spirit hath rejoiced in God my Saviour" (Luke 1:46-47).

Finally, rejoicing in His presence is preceded by beholding, yielding, trusting, and submitting to His transformative power in our lives. Design a plan today that will help you sense His Holiness, strength, and mercy daily (see Luke 1:49, 50). The Psalmist admonished, "Clap your hands, all you nations; shout to God with cries of joy. For the Lord Most High is awesome, the great King over all the earth. He subdued nations under us, peoples under our feet" (Psalm 47:1-3, NIV). "My lips will shout for joy when I sing praise to you—I whom you have delivered" (Psalm 71:23, NIV).

God is calling us to recognize that in His presence we will find joy, peace, and hope. He invites you to behold His majesty and purity, submit to Him, yield to Him, and rest quietly in His presence. He urges you to keep before you past victories and follow how He is leading you now. He desires that we dwell in His presence to experience stress-free living, confidence, and salvation.

*I surrender. I surrender to you. I acknowledge and move past my past experiences, troubles, and trama. All I want is you, and to focus on you. This transformation you are working on is big. Bigger than me, but I am ready. I am ready to serve you and love you more than anything in this world. You are my savior. Take me where you need me to go. I will follow. I will follow you to the ends of the earth.*

*Prepare for transformation. Serve our heavenly father. Do Gods work. I am here for a purpose. I may not understand my purpose yet, but I do know that I am a daughter of christ and I will always be his daughter.*

*Chapter 3*

# Keeping God's Purpose in Focus

"And she was in bitterness of soul, and prayed to the Lord and wept in anguish. Then she made a vow and said, 'O Lord of hosts, if You will indeed look on the affliction of Your maidservant and remember me, and not forget your maidservant, but will give Your maidservant a male child, then I will give him to the Lord all the days of his life...'" (1 Samuel 1:10, 11, NKJV).

Hannah was driven to prayer out of desperation. The Bible tells us that daily she was provoked, taunted, and attacked by Peninnah. Peninnah was a mean baby machine—every time Elkanah went in unto her, there was an egg waiting to be fertilized. However, Hannah's eggs were not fertile. Therefore, Peninnah made her miserable. She knew Hannah was vulnerable, her self-esteem was minimized by her lack of children, and she gained power from Hannah's weakness. She reminded Hannah daily that she was a disappointment and social disgrace. In that culture, to be childless meant that a woman did not fit into society and was looked on with disappointment. She intended that Hannah should feel that she did not fulfill God's destiny for her.

However, Hannah nurtured a burning desire in her heart to have a male child, and she refused to let it go until she had told the only One who could do something about it (see 1 Samuel 1:15). She believed that God had called her to a special purpose. Her intention was to fulfill that destiny. Thus, she used weapons that women are still using today—tears, passion, faith, and prayer. Her prayer is the first recorded prayer in the Bible that a woman prayed. She had a passion, purpose, and zeal to experience God's destiny for her. Therefore, she went into the temple with faith, passion, tears, and a prayer in her heart to see that destiny fulfilled.

Child of God, whatever the circumstances of your life may be, you are powerless to fix them. Take them to the Lord. *Develop a zeal and passion to fulfill God's destiny for you.* Pray a reckless prayer today. Like Hannah, pour out your heart and bitterness and weep before the Lord. Note that "Hannah spoke in her heart; only her lips moved, but her voice was not heard" (1 Samuel 1:13, NKJV). Only God should hear your desperate, reckless prayers. Then, after you have prayed recklessly before God, leave that scared place with peace in your heart, confident that God has answered your prayer. "So the woman went her way and ate, and her face was no longer sad" (1 Samuel 1:18, NKJV).

Then the woman engaged in family worship with her husband. They went home, and we are told that he knew her, and God remembered her reckless prayer, and in time God prepared a fertile egg and she bore a son and called his name Samuel, "Because I asked for him from the Lord."

Hannah kept her vow before the Lord and returned him to the temple to serve the Lord. Samuel later heard God's call and became a prophet in Israel. He anointed the first king of Israel. The trajectory of Hannah's experience was transformed from praying recklessly in tears and anguish to one of passionate praise and thanksgiving to God. Out of this transformation, she prayed, "My heart rejoices in the Lord; my horn is exalted in the Lord. I smile at my enemies because I rejoice in your salvation" (1 Samuel 2:1, NKJV).

Hannah's experience reminded me of a time in my life when I was overwhelmed with fear and uncertainty for my future and that of my children. One morning, during my devotion, I heard God saying, "Fear thou not for I am with you. Be not dismayed, for I am your God. Remember that I have plans to prosper you and not to harm you to give you hope and a future" (see Jeremiah 29:11). God drew me into ninety days of praying recklessly and passionately for guidance and clarity. At the end of that time with God, I knew with confidence the direction that I should follow.

My anxiety was transformed into peace, praise, thanksgiving, and confidence that God had a plan and was working it out for His glory.

During that time, though, I experienced uncertainty for the appropriate response that I should have, when God said to me, "What do you have in your hand?" This question plunged me deeper into the ninety-day prayer challenge with God. It helped me to better understand the direction that God was leading us. Throughout the ninety days, when I would inquire of God what I should do and what were His plans for my sons, He would respond, "What do you have in your hand?" Then, one day I realized what He was asking me. I said, "You know I am not going to do that, right? You will have to work it out some other way. No, I am not leaving my family to go anywhere." From that day, He was silent when I prayed and told Him my concerns. Nevertheless, I persisted in prayer. From 2001 to 2007, God was silent whenever I prayed for my children's future.

Meanwhile, my journey with God in prayer was taking an interesting turn. I awoke every day at 3:00 a.m., read the Bible, and discovered many hidden gems and promises that appealed to specific concerns and challenges that I was experiencing. I thanked God for leading me to the promise, prayed the promise, waited for God to respond, and thanked Him for answering my prayer. My prayer would follow this path: "Father, I come to you this morning because you said to call, and you will show me great and mighty things that I do not know. Lord, I do not know how to do this, what to do, or even how to move forward. Please instruct me and teach me and guide me with your eyes."

I found that praying the promises back to God and claiming them strengthened my faith and encouraged me. Every promise that I prayed and claimed was fulfilled that same day. I began praying recklessly every time I had a challenge and experienced God's transforming power in my life. I remember asking God for a plot of land to build a house. He reminded me of Luke 11:9–13: "ask, and it shall be given to you; seek, and ye shall find; knock, and it shall be opened unto you. For every one that asketh receiveth; and he that seeketh findeth; and to him that knocketh it shall be opened." One day, I fell into a deep sleep, and God showed me the plot of land in my dream and suggested how to proceed with constructing the house.

> *Calling to God and allowing Him to show us what we do not know suggests that God is omniscient, faithful, trustworthy, and reliable.*

Woman of God, what situation are you experiencing right now? Do you need to have children? Are you disappointed? Do you feel overwhelmed by your challenges? Are your children posing challenges? Are you experiencing problems in your marriage? Is another woman involved in your family life? Are you fearful for your future or that of your children? Do you feel God coaching you into an experience with Him?

Calling to God and allowing Him to show us what we do not know suggests that God is omniscient, faithful, trustworthy, and reliable. He knows what we need, what knowledge is important to our success and is able to guide us into paths that He wants us to go. When we call, it is important to trust Him, hold onto Him, accept His absolute truth, and open our eyes so that He may show us what we need to know to be successful.

**Our Prayer for Today:** Lord, I yield my mind to you today to be transformed by the power of your Holy Spirit. Take my anxiety, fears, and uncertainty and replace them with joy, peace, and praise. Magnify your power in my life and deliver me from my enemies. Amen!

*Chapter 4*
# *Experiencing His Possibility*

"For with God nothing will be impossible. Then Mary said, "behold the maidservant of the Lord! Let it be to me according to your word'" (Luke 1:37–38, NKJV).

Can you imagine the confusion in Mary's mind when the angel told her that she was going to have a baby? Mary was engaged to be married to Joseph. In those days, as it is now, that was a problematic and traumatic experience for a young woman and her family. The shame and embarrassment would not allow the marriage to take place. However, the angel reassured her that she was not alone, for Elizabeth, who had passed child-bearing age, was going to have a baby as well. Indeed, God specializes in impossibilities. He makes things happen that human minds cannot conceive. Mary could have decided 'I cannot do this. What will happen to my family or me?' Amidst all of the uncertainty, she was confident that God was in control and would take care of everything. She said, "Let it be to me according to your word." I am God's servant, and I will do whatever He says. Mary's response indicated a total commitment to God and reliance on His providence. She demonstrated an attitude of joy in His presence and belief in His plan.

## Chapter 4  Experiencing His Possibility

After Mary had submitted to God in prayer, she uttered songs of adoration and prayerful rejoicing. She praised God with her soul and spirit when she exclaimed, "My soul magnifies the Lord, and my spirit has rejoiced in God my Savior" (Luke 1:46–47, NKJV). Mary acknowledged that God's greatness, power, and might was manifested in her life.

Women of God, the secret to experiencing God's power in your life is a total surrender to His will and embracing His destiny for your life. Then you will receive showers of mercy and blessings. He will lift you up if you are humble, trusting, devoted, consecrated, confident, and pure in spirit. He was with Mary throughout her pregnancy, protecting her, providing for her, turning her impending shame into a positive experience, and throughout the experience with Jesus as He grew. He remained with her at the cross and thereafter. God is the same yesterday, today, and forevermore. He always will and ever will be. We can trust Him.

Later, when Jesus was grown and about to conduct His first miracle, Mary told the servants, "Whatever He says to you do it" (John 2:5, NKJV). What she was saying, I have personal experiences with trusting Him. The result will be powerful. Many times in our lives, what God is asking us to do may not sound reasonable, but we can be confident that if He tells us to do it, He knows the result. During these times when He is revealing the plans and purposes for our lives, we can say with praise and assurance, "Lord! Let it be to me according to your word" (Luke 1:38, NKJV). Thus, we can do with all our energy what He is asking us to do.

Mary was the first recorded woman in the Bible to say the words, "Let it be done according to your word." Through this expression of confidence in God, she demonstrated the attitude of every woman who allows God to direct her life. Woman of God, if you are waiting for Him to fulfill His intention for your life, then, "Whatever He says to you do it." When God makes a request of you, fall on your knees and, like Mary, declare, "Lord! Let it be to me according to your word." Then, rejoice in His presence with the knowledge that He is hearing and answering your prayers.

**Our prayer today:** Lord, I acknowledge that nothing is impossible with you. I surrender my life, heart, soul, and spirit into your hands and yield my will to you. I accept your plan for my life, so lead me to the path that you want to take me. Then, when God manifests His power in your life, shout praise, thanksgiving, and joy for what He has done for you. Amen!

*Chapter 5*

# Experiencing His Intervention

"Then Esther told them to reply to Mordecai;' 'Go gather all the Jews who are present in Shushan, and fast for me; neither eat nor drink for three days, night or day; my maids and I will fast likewise. And so I will go to the king, which is against the law; and if I perish I perish'" (Esther 4:15–16, NKJV)!

It was a time of tremendous anxiety, fear, confusion, and uncertainty. The decree was issued—all must bow down to Haman or be annihilated. Men and women cried, worried, panicked, and went into mourning. Esther had just been chosen as queen and had to wait her turn to go into the king's chambers when the news of Haman's intent was delivered to her. She feared for her life; she could not go to the king without being summoned. With the fate of the entire nation in her hands, she decided to fast and pray for three days, then go to the king. Esther used the weapons that all women use when confronted with challenges—prayer, fasting, trust, faith, wisdom, charm, and holy boldness. Esther invited Israel to fast and pray recklessly with faith and confidence in God's ability to deliver them from destruction.

## Chapter 5 Experiencing His Intervention 21

The time spent with God was so powerful that when Esther entered the king's palace, the Shekinah glory enshrouded her and the king just had to extend the golden scepter. It was so powerful that her winning charm, beauty, and poise made her irresistible to the king. Esther invited the king and Haman to a banquet—we have heard it said the way to a man's heart is through his stomach—then she made her request. He was willing to grant her request even if she wanted half the kingdom.

God has a way of entering into desperate situations and turning them around. While Haman was plotting his spate of destruction, God miraculously intervened and reminded the king that Mordecai had saved his life. The king responded by directing the one who wanted to destroy Israel to honor Mordecai. When the plot to destroy Mordecai and Israel was unmasked, the king ordered that Haman be hanged on the very gallows that he built for Mordecai. God magnified Esther, Mordecai, and Israel in front of their enemies. He restored the dignity and peacefulness of all Israel. The trajectory of the experiences of Esther, Mordecai, and all Israel was transformed as a result of prayer, fasting, trust, wisdom, and unselfishness.

> *God has a way of entering into desperate situations and turning them around.*

Woman of God, you are blessed with beauty, charm, poise, and confidence, not for the edification of yourself, but to fulfill your divine destiny. Esther was willing to die to save her people. She knew that with fasting and prayer, the king would extend his hand. God is calling you to step outside of your self-centeredness and sense of inadequacy and plunge yourself into His holy hands for protection, to experience transformation and restoration. God wants to magnify you before your enemies and those who are seeking to destroy you. He wants to use you to bring peace to desperate and anxious situations. He wants to transform the trajectory of your daily experiences. Do you know if you have come to this place for such a time as this? Is this your mountain or valley of transformation?

**Our Prayer for Today**: Lord, I yield my mind to you today that you may fill me with your spirit, so that I may relinquish my inadequacy and embrace your power to bring peace, transformation, and salvation to others. Amen!

*Chapter 6*
# Faithfulness in Prayer Yields Rewards

"And she coming in that instant gave thanks likewise unto the Lord, and spake of him to all them that looked for redemption in Jerusalem" (Luke 2:38).

How do you feel when God answers your prayers? Do you clap your hands and shout praises and thanksgiving to Him? In the story of Anna, we experience what it means to abide in God's presence and be faithful in adversity. She was a young woman when her husband of seven years died. She remained faithful for eighty-four years. She dwelled in the temple, consistently served God, fasted, and prayed night and day (see Luke 2:36–37). Just picture the scene and experience the depth of Anna's tenacity in prayer. Scripture suggests that she prayed for the coming Messiah. She recognized the Messiah the instant she saw Him. She ushered her presence into the temple with resounding prayers and triumphant shouts of joy. Anna had finally experienced the fulfillment of her prayers.

Her consistent, daily prayers were rewarded with the sight of this new baby in His mother's arms. This triumphant moment was the fulfillment of prophecy. Men and women waited in eager anticipation for this moment to come where they would be restored to fellowship with God. Anna was indeed a prodigy of destiny. She exemplified wisdom, trust, faith, perseverance, and commitment to the hope of the coming Messiah and His mission. She lived faithfully in the temple daily with her eyes fixed on God's destiny for her. The tenacity in the hope that she had for seeing the coming Messiah was rewarded that day.

God rewarded Anna's faithfulness in prayer with the privilege of seeing the Savior. Her attitude in prayer provides a clear indication of how we are to persevere in prayer. When God lays a challenge on our hearts, we are to fast and pray with confidence in His ability to bring it to pass. It may be that we are praying for our children, husband, or deliverance. Anna's experience in the temple reminds us that we are to meet God day and night in our temples. We are to serve God faithfully and approach His temple in faith with the belief that He will hear us. Experiencing God's answer to our prayers requires tenacity and intense commitment to the hope that lies within us to see the fulfillment of His promise to us. He is faithful to His promises and will always answer our faithful prayer.

**Our Prayer for Today**: Dear God, give me the strength to be faithful and help me to abide in your temple daily.

> *Experiencing God's answer to our prayers requires tenacity and intense commitment to the hope that lies within us to see the fulfillment of His promise to us.*

*Chapter 7*

# *Experiencing His Healing: The Great Exchange*

Our willingness to transfer our anxieties, uncertainties, and sorrows to the Lord will result in lasting emotional healing. The Bible cites many examples of individuals who experienced emotional healing by transferring their emotional pains to the Lord through prayer. One such example was Hezekiah. He went into the temple and "spread" his burden before the Lord (see 2 Kings 19:14–15). To spread a burden before the Lord means to acknowledge one's dependence upon the Lord. James calls this "spreading" of burdens "casting" them upon the Lord. God cares for us. Therefore, He invites us to "cast" or "spread" our anxieties upon Him. It is said that the Lord gives "beauty for ashes."

In Isaiah 61:3, the prophet views emotional healing as an act of reciprocity. Isaiah says God gives us emotional healing by engaging us in acts of emotional exchanges. In these emotional exchanges, the Lord gives us "beauty for ashes," "the oil of joy for mourning," and the "garment of praise for heaviness." The Lord gives us beauty, joy, and praise in exchange for our ashes, mourning, and spirit of heaviness. This is a beautiful image of emotional healing. Such healing comes from our willingness

## Chapter 7 Experiencing His Healing: The Great Exchange

to spread or cast all our anxieties upon the Lord so He may give us His peace and joy.

In Psalm 30:5, the psalmist purports that emotional healing is an act of anticipating joy while still experiencing sorrow or anguish. The condition of our minds matters in the process of emotional healing. If we expect that joy will come in the "morning" to replace our night of "weeping", then the joyful state of our minds affects emotional health. Indeed, emotional healing is based on the principle of exchange. Joy replaces weeping as day replaces night. Therefore, emotional healing is an act of anticipating happiness while still experiencing anxiety, grief, uncertainty, and disappointment.

As a man, Jesus maintained His emotional health. He anticipated the "joy that was set before him [and] endured the cross, despising the shame..." (Hebrews 12:2). Jesus allowed His mind to dwell on things which were noble and lofty. Therefore, the focus of His mind influenced His emotional health.

In Psalm 126:5–6, the psalmist expands on the idea of emotional health in ministry. He states, "they that sow in tears shall reap in joy." This is because joy existed before tears. Joy is permanent. Our tears are temporal. This means that emotional healing is the result of patience during times of anxiety, uncertainty, and grief. We are to cultivate patience during difficult times in ministry. This is because all difficult times do come to an end. We should view times of difficulties as temporal occurrences—"this too will come to pass." How we interpret the times of anxieties and uncertainties affects our emotional health. Therefore, the Psalmist argues that we should interpret every difficulty in ministry as temporal. Jesus transitions us from "sowing in tears" to "reaping in joy."

> *The condition of our minds matters in the process of emotional healing. If we expect that joy will come in the "morning" to replace our night of "weeping", then the joyful state of our minds affects emotional health.*

Intercessory prayer is the medium by which we can "spread", "cast", "exchange", or transition our needs to the Lord. Prayer is like a vehicle which transports goods from one place to another. Through prayer, we transfer our burdens to the Lord, so that He may give us His joy, assurance, hope, peace, and happiness. Emotional healing is a gift from God. We need to ask God to give us emotional healing. However, we must first be willing to give the Lord our ashes for His beauty; our mourning for His joy; and our anxiety for His garment of praise. Then we shall experience emotional healing to the glory of the Lord and the blessing of others.

In Ephesians 4:31–32, Paul considers emotional healing as an act of forgiveness. He argues that we should forgive others to the extent that Christ has forgiven us. John, the beloved apostle, says, "if we confess our sins, he is faithful and just to forgive us our sins" (1 John 1:9). This is because sin causes guilt and guilt disturbs our emotional balance. When Jesus forgives our sins, He removes our guilt also. This means forgiveness and removal of guilt restore our emotional balance. Therefore, emotional healing is a gift from God. Indeed, emotional healing is a gift of grace. Grace is pardon for sin. Jesus died that we might receive grace, which is pardon for sin.

Paul argues that having received forgiveness from Christ, we should also be we willing to forgive others. Paul views forgiveness as an act of sharing God's grace with others. You have freely received God's grace; therefore, you should choose to extend His grace freely to others. "Freely ye have received, freely give" (Mathew 10:8). Since we receive forgiveness as a gift of grace, we should be willing to extend forgiveness to others who have caused us grief, pain, and anguish.

Paul believes that emotional healing is like changing of one's garment. He uses the phrases "putting away" and "putting on" to convey the idea that emotional healing means a change in one's emotional condition. Paul urges us to "put away" all bitterness, wrath, anger, clamor, all malice, and evil speaking. Paul uses emotive words to paint a picture of a dirty garment or negative emotion. This type of garment/emotion must be put away from us. Paul invites us to "put on" a new type of emotional garment. He describes the emotional garment as kindness, tenderness, and forgiveness. It is a new type of emotional garment. It is a gift from God. Paul believes that emotional healing is a transition from an old emotional garment to a new emotional garment in Christ Jesus.

In Proverbs 18:14, Solomon states that "spirit of man will sustain him in sickness" (NKJV). What does Solomon mean by the spirit of man? The phrase "spirit of man" conveys the meaning of a positive or healthy emotion. The "spirit of man" also conveys the idea of a healthy disposition toward anxieties, uncertainties, and frustrations. A healthy disposition would include resilience, faith in divine power, perseverance and emotional stability. This "spirit of the man" gives us the internal fortitude to

# Chapter 7 Experiencing His Healing: The Great Exchange

cope with external events such as sickness, grief, uncertainties, anxieties, and disappointments.

Emotional healing is a strong fortress against the stresses of life. Ellen G. White states,

"We are in a world of suffering. Difficulty, trial, and sorrow await us all along the way to the heavenly home. But there are many who make life's burdens doubly heavy by continually anticipating trouble. If they meet with adversity or disappointment they think that everything is going to ruin, that theirs is the hardest lot of all, that they are surely coming to want. Thus they bring wretchedness upon themselves and cast a shadow upon all around them. Life itself becomes a burden to them. But it need not be thus. It will cost a determined effort to change the current of their thought. But the change can be made. Their happiness, both for this life and for the life to come, depends upon their fixing their minds upon cheerful things. Let them look away from the dark picture, which is imaginary, to the benefits which God has strewn in their pathway, and beyond these to the unseen and eternal" (*Ministry of Healing*, p. 136).

**Our Prayer for Today**: Dear God, help me to recognize Your purpose in my life. I surrender my will and desires to you. Please guide me to live in your grace.

*Chapter 8*

# Releasing the Problem to Him

"And Hezekiah received the letter from the hand of the messengers, and read I;, and Hezekiah went up to the house of the Lord and spread it before the Lord" (Isaiah 37:14, NKJV).

Problems could be such heavy burdens that they destroy our minds, bodies, and souls. If we try to bear these burdens alone, they could alienate us from God, family, and society. As Christians, we need to recognize that we do not have the wisdom to solve our problems. God has the resources to deal with every problem that we will ever encounter. We can simply release our problems to Him.

Hezekiah received the letter from his powerful enemy Sennacherib, but he did not worry or stress. "He went up to the house of the Lord and spread it before the Lord" (Isaiah 37:14). He recognized that he was powerless and that God had the solution to this problem. The path to victory over the mighty army of Sennacherib could only be discovered in one place. Hezekiah went to the temple of God's presence and spread the letter before God. Then the king prayed to God who has all the real answers.

Our prayer lives will be transformed if we pay attention to several important elements in Hezekiah's prayer. The king recognized that God is in charge of everything and everyone. "O Lord of hosts, God of Israel, the One, who dwells between the cherubim, You are God, You alone, of all the kingdoms of the earth" (Isaiah 37:16, NKJV). Hezekiah declared that he knew God and believed in His sovereignty. Hezekiah acknowledged the problem before God. Then, he presented his request to the King of the universe. "Now, therefore, O Lord, our God, save us from his hand, that all the kingdoms of the earth may know that You are the Lord, You alone"(Isaiah 37:20, NKJV).

Hezekiah's approach to his enormous problem demonstrates the power of releasing every challenge to God. Every difficulty is a prayer challenge, and God never runs away from a challenge. He specializes in challenges. He wants us to come to Him, call out to Him, and spread out our troubles before Him. He asks us to surrender every challenge to Him. Israel did not have to fight against Sennacharib and his army. The angel of the Lord fought for His people, and the victory was complete. Hezekiah prayed, and the Lord responded. The man of God said, "He shall not come into this city, nor shoot an arrow there, nor come before it with shield, nor build a siege mound against it. By the way he came, by the same shall he return; And he shall not come into this city; says the Lord, for I will defend this city, to save it for my sake and my servant David's sake" (Isaiah 37:33–35, NKJV). Israel turned the problem over to God, followed His directions, and experienced victory.

Women of God, no problem that confronts you is too big for God to solve. Every difficulty is a prayer challenge. When we are surrounded by powerful individuals or massive problems, follow Hezekiah's example. Spread the situation before God. Release the weight of it, "Casting all your care upon him; for he cares for you" (1 Peter 5:7). Recognize that God has all the necessary power at His disposal to solve your problem, and He will solve it in ways that we cannot possibly imagine.

There was a time in my life when I encountered a terrible situation in which I was powerless to solve the problem. There was no way out. I could not rise against my persecutors. Instantly I turned to God. I lifted the document to the Lord, called to Him, and told Him what my request was. While I was yet speaking, God heard my prayer, and in a few minutes, the problem was solved. The promise in Jeremiah 29:11 ("For I know the thoughts that I think toward you, saith the Lord, thoughts of peace, and not of evil, to give you an expected end") became real in my life.

God is sovereign over all and can destroy the army that is pursuing us. He can transfer that boss who is pressuring us; He can transform that child or husband who is causing problems in our lives. He can condemn the words of people and destroy their weapons. He can turn away the darts that are pointed in our direction. He is able. All we need to do is trust Him to accept our challenges when we spread them before Him. He will defend us for His own name's sake and solve the problem.

**Our Prayer for Today**: Lord, who dwells in the heavens, You are God. Every power belongs to You. Listen and see this problem by which I am surrounded and save me from the hands of my persecutors. Lord, I leave this problem in your hand and wait for you to take care of it.

*Chapter 9*

# *Experiencing His Power*

"For we have no power against this great multitude that is coming against us; nor do we know what to do, but our eyes are upon you" (2 Chronicles 20:12, NKJV).

Picture the scene: a mighty, powerful army is coming towards you. Its only intention is to destroy you and everyone else. You look around and recognize that your weapons are antiquated and your army seems incapable. The natural human reaction is to panic. We read that "Jehoshaphat feared, and set himself to seek the Lord, and proclaimed a fast throughout all Judah. And Judah gathered themselves together, to ask help of the Lord: even out of all the cities of Judah they came to seek the Lord" (2 Chronicles 20:3–4).

Jehoshaphat's fear did not last long. He proclaimed a fast throughout all Judah in preparation to unite forces with the army of God. Notice the process in which they were engaged. Fear is a natural human reaction to impending attack from the enemy, but Jehoshaphat did not allow it to linger or cripple his response. He turned to God. There was no time for anxiety and panic; an army was quickly approaching, and that required a swift response. The prayer that followed provides a clear picture of how we are to pray when confronted with impending danger. Many times in our daily experiences we are challenged by people who may think that they are more powerful than we are, but Jehoshaphat's experience provides a vivid reminder that God is the source of power and might. He will protect and defend us in every situation, for the battle is always His battle. If we would trust Him in every situation, we will not have to fight with our words, fists, or even allow fear to consume us.

> *Many times in our daily experiences we are challenged by people who may think that they are more powerful than we are, but Jehoshaphat's experience provides a vivid reminder that God is the source of power and might.*

Every situation should be a prayer challenge that beckons us to recognize God's sovereignty. He is the God of yesterday and today. He rules over all, even the impending army. All power is in His hands, and no one can withstand His might. The defense that He performed yesterday, He can perform today. He is able and willing. In trying times, all God requires of us is a total surrender of the problem to Him. That is exactly what Jehoshaphat did. His prayer is one of recognizing who God is, His power, majesty, and how He delivered in the past, thus prompting us to believe that He will hear and answer our prayers in the present.

Our kindness to others in the past may translate into destruction in the present. It is a challenging situation when we realize that people who we treated kindly are seeking our destruction. Nevertheless, we need always to remember that we are powerless to defend ourselves before others who may think that they are stronger than we are. In situations like these, we need to proclaim, like Jehoshaphat, "For we have no power against this great multitude that is coming against us; nor do we know what to do, but our eyes *are* upon You" (2 Chronicles 20:12, NKJV). Notice that Israel entered the presence of God and focused on His power to defend them.

They became a captive audience of the almighty God. In His presence, they were focused on His might, power, and past victories. In this scenario, they became active listeners. Women of God, when we are challenged and surrounded on every side, we need not look to the sides with fear, but rather look up, for it is from above that help will descend. The battle, the challenge, the intended evil is not ours to fight. It is the Lord's.

If we would just stop, pray, fast, turn the problem over to Him, listen, and wait, we will experience deliverance. Victory in every challenging situation belongs to God. We need not fear and worry, for God is able. He performed past successes in our lives, and He will do it again. He will deliver us.

Praise and thanksgiving should follow a prayer for deliverance. The mingling of praise and thanksgiving with a prayer for deliverance releases the stress from our minds and acknowledges God's power to deliver. In an attitude of praise and thanksgiving, we experience deliverance from the enemy. In an attitude of praise and thanksgiving, many battles are won. When the challenge is turned over to God with implicit confidence in His power to fight for us, we can sing praise and thanksgiving to Him. We can experience deliverance and peace.

The army of Israel did not have to fight, for the enemy defeated itself. Our enemies will defeat themselves. They will begin fighting against each other. They will be so confused that they will destroy themselves. In your challenges, you do not have to fight. Even before the battle begins God dispatches His army to deliver you. He beckons you to take your eyes off the ground and sides and look up, for above the ground is power, victory, and deliverance.

Deliverance from destruction should result in praise and thanksgiving. When we experience deliverance from destruction, we should rejoice in God's presence. We need to leave the place of victory with peace in our hearts for the success that we achieved and the battles that we did not have to fight. God can fight our battles and win them. His army is the most powerful, and no one can stand against Him. After the deliverance, Israel went to Jerusalem with stringed instruments and rejoicing for what God had done for them.

**Our Prayer for Today**: Oh great and mighty God, who rules over the heavens and earth. All power and might are in your hands. We recognize how you protected us in the past, and we come with implicit faith and confidence in your power to fight this battle for us. I place this problem, individual, or situation in your hands. I have no might or power against this situation or person, but my trust and confidence are in Your ability to deliver me. I am waiting, listening, and trusting You to fight for me. My eyes are set on you, Lord, for I know that You can and will deliver me. Thank you, God, for deliverance. I praise You for deliverance, and I surrender my life to walk in Your will.

## Chapter 10
# *Experiencing His Deliverance*

"And I set my face unto the Lord God, to seek by prayer and supplications, with fasting, and sackcloth, and ashes: And I prayed unto the Lord my God, and made my confession, and said, O Lord, the great and dreadful God, keeping the covenant and mercy to them that love him, and to them that keep his commandments; We have sinned, and have committed iniquity, and have done wickedly, and have rebelled, even by departing from thy precepts and from thy judgments" (Daniel 9:3–5).

Many challenges confront the Christian every day, and our response to these challenges could determine our quality of life. Is there a special way to pray? We may talk to God while walking, standing, or on our knees. The nature of the prayer and our location will determine the exact posture for prayer. If we are driving along the highway, one will not expect that we close our eyes. We may continue driving and talk to God. In Daniel's context, the situation was dangerous; Israel was in captivity and needed God's intervention urgently.

In this story, we learn several important points of how we may approach God when there is a need for deliverance. Note that Daniel "set his face to the Lord to make his request." It is important to set your face, mind, and heart towards God. Your thoughts must center on God during your prayers. The posture observed in prayer is essential to the connection that one experiences during prayer.

Another important thing that Daniel did was fast. Fasting may be complete eating no solid food, but drinking water during the time of prayer. One may decide to eat fruits and drink water. In Daniel's case, he ate vegetables. The idea for fasting during prayer for intervention is to avoid solid food. For health reasons, one may fast from one meal. Before beginning the fast, you need to decide what kind of fast and the length of the fast to which God is leading you. Gather all of the ingredients and proceed to begin the fast. Also, plan to spend time reading the Word, meditating, listening to God speak to you through the Word, and pray the Word back to God. Fasting frees the mind and allows the focus to be on God and away from oneself. It is a powerful form of worship to God.

In this subdued sense of connection with God, one recognizes the greatness and awesomeness of God. His mercy and love become real. In this sense of realness, confession allows us to experience humility in God's presence. We recognize our sinfulness and need for forgiveness. The details of our sins spread before us in a panoramic vision, and we cry out to God to forgive our particular sins. In the eyes of the sinner, only God is righteous and can forgive sins. He sees our disobedience and unlawfulness. Therefore, when we pray to God for intervention, it is important that we tell Him our deepest secrets and spill our wrongdoing before Him, for it is only in this state that God can hear and answer us. Only when we empty ourselves can we experience His healing, forgiveness, and restoration.

*Many challenges confront the Christian every day, and our response to these challenges could determine our quality of life.*

Daniel cried out to God and asked Him to hear his prayer and see the situation. He said, "hear and forgive, listen and act." He was appealing to God's cognition and vision. You see, God is always aware of our situations, but He needs us to come to Him, confess, and humble ourselves before Him. It is in these humble states of mind that God can help us in every situation. We must recognize our desperation and inability to change our situations. This posture beckons us to rely entirely on God for help.

Daniel knew what he was praying for before he began. Note, he recognized God's mercy and love, confessed his sins and those of the people, asked for forgiveness, made his requests known to God, and pleaded that

God would help them in the desperate situation. He said, "Oh Lord hear, forgive, listen, and act," for these people are Your people, help them for Your sake. He appealed to God's fatherly instinct and desire to help His children.

Women of God, we can learn a lot from Daniel's experience with God. First things first: clear, specific confession is necessary. This allows us to humble ourselves before God and let His transforming power permeate our beings. Then, fasting allows lasting spiritual blessings to remain with us even after the fast. The challenges over which you needed victories will burst through the thick darkness with which the enemy surrounded you, and God's glory will be revealed to you. Your thinking will become clearer, and God's will and direction will become evident.

**Our Prayer for Today:** Oh great, awesome, mighty God, have mercy on us. We have sinned before you and committed such and such sin. We recognize that you alone are righteous. We come to you, asking you to look down upon us, hear us, forgive us, and act on our request. Help us, God, not for ourselves, but that Your Great Name will be magnified. We thank You for hearing and answering our prayer. Amen!

*Chapter 11*
# Submitting to His Transformation

"Then I will sprinkle clean water on you, and you shall be clean; I will cleanse you from all your filthiness and all your idols. I will give you a new heart and put a new spirit within you; I will take the heart of stone out of your flesh and give you a heart of flesh. I will put my spirit with-in you and cause you to walk in my statutes, and you will keep my judgments and do them" (Ezekiel 36:25–27, NKJV).

I wash dishes every day; if the sink is full, I place them in the dishwasher. However, there are times that I wash small amounts in the sink. I would fill the sink with water and dishwashing liquid or just allow the water to flow from the faucet over these dishes while I wash them. Either way, the dirty dishes are clean after experiencing the rush, flow, or sprinkling of the water over them. This act of washing dishes reminds me of the transforming power of the Holy Spirit.

God positions His Holy Spirit over our beings to cleanse us from our filthiness—our lying, gossiping, jealousy, negative thinking, unforgiving hearts—in order to transform us into a clean vessel. The new experience of the Holy Spirit within us causes us to be loving, forgiving, positive thinkers and guides our tongues to speak positive words. Then we will walk in His way, obey His commandments, and live by the principles in His words.

He promises to take away our stony hearts and give us hearts of flesh. The term "heart" suggests that the heart is the center of thinking, reasoning, desires, and actions. The promise here reassures us of God's transforming power in our lives. He is the only one who could perform a heart transplant of this magnitude.

This transformation takes place when the sinner recognizes his/her sinful state and submits to God for cleansing. He willingly performs the transformative surgery on the heart. The process is straightforward and painless. The sinner thus transformed from the inside, can now obey His commands, walk in His statutes, and minister to others who are trapped in satan's nets.

Woman of God, are you stuck in negative experiences? God is calling you today to surrender all of your negative experiences to Him and experience His transforming power. He is ready to sprinkle or pour the clean, fresh power of His Holy Spirit into your mind, soul, and heart to transform you. Whatever the situation, God can and is waiting to change you. Ellen G. White says that God is willing to come to you if you would just submit your soul unto His transforming power. Why not talk to God right now? Ask Him to pour the transforming power of His Holy Spirit over your mind, soul, and heart and flush everything that is not of His will out of you. Then rest in His arms and experience the cleansing power of His Holy Spirit. The experience is miraculous and uplifting.

God is faithful to His promises and is waiting for us to come unto Him just as we are. Imagine standing under a shower of the Holy Spirit that is reaching into your heart and flushing everything that is hindering God's grace from blessing you. It happens in a moment, and then you are transformed by the power of the Holy Spirit. You leave the "shower" feeling refreshed and empowered. There is a pep in your step and joy on your face. God has just rescued one sinner from the enemy's camp.

It is only when God's power is within you that He can work through you to change your situation. The transformation will result in restoration of everything that the enemy tried to take away from you. A new heart, new spirit, and new thinking will be placed in you to enable you. Today if you hear His voice, harden not your heart. Restoration is an imminent and positive response to surrender. Trust yourself to God's grace and mercy and experience His desire to restore and redeem you.

**Our Prayer for Today**: Dear God, I come to You today with all of my weaknesses and challenges. I surrender my heart, spirit, and being to You.

Pour the fresh anointing of Your Spirit on me and in me. Flush everything from me that is hindering Your power from manifesting in my life. Replace these negative things with Your peace, joy, and power. Help me to be an instrument of Your grace and mercy to others to lead them into a restored relationship with You. Amen!

*Chapter 12*

# Basking in His Ability to Restore

"Ah Lord God! behold, thou hast made the heaven and the earth by thy great power and stretched out arm, and there is nothing too hard for thee… Behold, I am the Lord, the God of all flesh: is there any thing too hard for me" (Jeremiah 32:17, 27)?

Have you ever found yourself in a situation where you needed clarity and understanding? In spite of the fuzziness of the situation, you knew it was going to work out. Did you know deep down in your heart that God was in control in spite of the confusion? God is all-powerful and can make all things happen. Nothing is too hard for Him to do. He is in charge of everything and knows the end from the beginning. He has the plan to restore all that you've lost.

Judah's transgressions caused pain, confusion, and sorrow to descend on Isreal. However, God had a plan to restore His children. Zedekiah was not happy with the message from God, so he placed the messenger in prison. Jeremiah was confused. God sent him to warn Israel, but they locked him away in prison. The drama began unfolding when God told Jeremiah to buy the property from Hanameel and preserve the deed for prosperity. It became apparent that the dream was of the Lord and he responded positively to God's command. Moreover, Jeremiah recognized God's power to restore and poured out adoration and praise to God with hope, trust, and confidence in His ability to restore everything that Judah lost. We can never drift too far from God for His power to reach us. He may allow us to experience pain because of our mistakes, but He has the authority to restore us. Even before we drift away, God has a plan to restore us if we submit and return to Him. Note that Jeremiah was instructed to buy the land and preserve the deed before Nebuchadnezzar captured Isreal. Then God directed him toward the action that he should take during the captivity. Jeremiah experienced the power of God to do everything for His children. Judah was taken into captivity as God told Jeremiah. They endured the pain and suffering of their disobedience, but God restored them. "Behold, He is the God of all flesh, there is nothing too hard for Him to do." In every difficulty, we are to recognize that He is the only one who could transform our situations into positive ones.

Many times, in the confusion that we may have caused, we suffer, but God said in His Word, if we surrender, repent, and trust Him, He will restore us. Jeremiah cried out to God, saying, "I know they have not obeyed your voice in spite of all that you did for them. Now, look at what is happening to your children. The enemies have descended on them to take them away and occupy the city that you gave to your children. You told me to buy the land and secure it for them, yet someone else is occupying it." God responded, "Behold, I am the Lord, the God of all flesh: is there any thing too hard for me" (Jeremiah 32:27).

> *Woman of God, even if your situation is hopeless, God has the power to restore you to His planned destiny for your life.*

He further said, "And I will make an everlasting covenant with them, that I will not turn away from them, to do them good; but I will put my fear in their hearts, that they shall not depart from me. Yea, I will rejoice over them to do them good, and I will plant them in this land assuredly with my whole heart and with my whole soul" (Jeremiah 32:40, 41). He will restore everything that we've lost up to a hundredfold, or far beyond our imaginations. God is all-powerful; there is nothing too hard for Him to do. He just requires that we submit to His leading, laws, and transformational power.

Woman of God, even if your situation is hopeless, God has the power to restore you to His planned destiny for your life. Is your condition dark right now? Are you feeling helpless and hopeless? Have you drifted from where God wanted you to be? Are you confused, wondering, or unable to understand your situation? The God of all flesh is powerful. He can transform your situation right now. Why not stop reading and tell Him what you do not understand. Tell Him your concerns, challenges, problems, confusions—tell Him everything. You can tell Him everything. He will never share with anyone else. You can be confident that your situation and story are safe with the all-powerful God. Nothing is too hard for Him to do, even keeping your issue secure.

Judah was in captivity, but God went there with them. He never abandoned them. The almighty God is present in our situations, even when it appears dark, so dark that we cannot see beyond the thick blackness. The darkness may be so dense that we can feel it, but God is there. Nothing is too hard for Him to do. He will bring you out of captivity and restore what you have lost beyond your imagination. God primed Jeremiah for the decision to purchase the property. He had a plan for its preservation for Israel's inheritance. He reclaimed His chosen people and placed His laws in their hearts. He purposed to keep them under His feathers and save them eternally.

Pray this prayer with me right now. Almighty powerful Father, You show lovingkindness to many and cause the pain of the parents to visit their children. God, You are great in wisdom, and Your eyes are opened for all Your children to see everything that troubles them. Father, I believe nothing is too hard for You to do. I submit to Your cleansing, forgiveness, and restoration. Please forgive me for my sins and restore my life, family, and joy. Hear my cry and answer my prayers.

Tell God Your challenges, concerns, and needs right now.

## Chapter 13
# *Pathways to God's Blessings*

"Moreover, Jabez called on the God of Israel, saying, 'Oh that you bless me indeed, and enlarge my territory, that Your hand would be with me, and that You would keep me from evil, that I may not cause pain,' so God granted him what he requested" (1 Chronicles 4:10, NKJV).

A few years ago, when my family worked for the Caribbean Union, my husband served as prayer coordinator, and he invited Ruthie Jacobson—she was the prayer coordinator for the North American Division—to conduct a prayer conference. Her focus for that conference was the "Prayer of Jabez." I had read the book of 1 Chronicles but never paid much attention to the prayer. Many individuals who attended the prayer conference began studying the prayer and praying it.

Heather-Dawn Small was one of those individuals. Sister Small took this prayer to another level. She prayed it, intentionally believing that God would hear and answer her prayers. One day, a friend who worked at the General Conference told her of the need for a Women's Ministries Director at the General Conference. She applied for the position, and today, God is blessing her and enlarging her territory.

When we ask God to bless us and enlarge our territories, He responds positively. At times, we may receive His blessings and travel the world and meet many people enlarge the territory in the literal sense of the word. At other occasions, we may bless others who continue to be a blessing to many that you may never reach, thus expanding your influence and acknowledging God's blessings in your life.

Let us examine Jabez's prayer. In verse 9 of chapter 4, we read, "And Jabez was more honourable than his brethren: and his mother called his name Jabez, saying, Because I bare him with sorrow." Could you imagine naming your son because of the pain associated with the birth of that child? Maybe the pain was more intense than at the birth of the other kids. We do not know. In spite of the pain or negative connotations of his name, we are told that he "was more honourable than his brethren." Jabez must have recognized that God was the only one who could transform his situation and life. The word "indeed" comes after "bless" and suggests that Jabez desired God to bless him positively, sincerely, and fairly. Today, it might read, 'Lord I am asking you to bless me.' He did not stop at asking for the blessing but asked God to connect him with many people so that he may share the benefits with them. When God blesses us, it is not for us to sit quietly by and live out our lives on the beach or swinging in a hammock. The life that is blessed is a life that God rewards. Therefore, we are to share them with others so that they too will be blessed. In the prayer, Jabez continued to ask God to keep His hands on him and keep/preserve him from evil so that others may not experience pain. This is important, for the empowering and blessing process is intended for us to continue to minister. We should ever be cognizant that God's intention for blessing us is to bless others, thus, transforming their lives. In the book *Prayer* is the claim that "We are to ask blessings from God that we may communicate to others. The capacity for receiving is preserved only by imparting. We cannot continue to receive heavenly treasure without communicating to those around us" (White, p. 307, 2002). The blessing process is not intended to empower us to hurt others. It is destined to change lives positively and continue the process of consecration. The verse ends by saying, "so God granted him what he requested."

Let's examine the conditions that preceded the blessing. (1) bless me magnificently, Lord. (2) Enlarge my territory or sphere of influence. (3) Keep your hand/anointing on me. (4) preserve me from evil. (5) Help me not to cause pain. Then God granted him the desire for blessings. From the essence of the texts, I perceive that Jabez believed that God is a rewarder of those who go to Him in faith. In Hebrews 11:6, we read, "But without faith it is impossible to please Him, for he who comes to God must believe that He is, and that He is a rewarder of those who diligently seek Him" (NKJV). It took faith for Jabez to ask God to bless him sincerely and then anoint him to the extent that he will be a blessing to others and not cause them any pain. Therefore, if we desire God to bless us, we must believe that He is able and will do what we ask Him. Another essential ingredient for receiving God's blessings is keeping our connection with Him strong. God will not bless the one who is not connected to Him. If He blesses you outside of Him, what will you do? He desires that you remain connected to Him. In John 15:4, we read that if we abide in God, He will bear fruit through us. In Matthew 12:33, we are admonished that God will transform our lives if we abide in Him. You are to decide that from today forward you will remain connected to Him. Therefore, if we claim to live in Jesus, we must abide in Him. Then our lives will be transformed from ordinary to extraordinary. He wants to enlarge your territory so that you may share/transmit the blessings that He has bestowed on you to others. In his book, *Secrets of the Vine*, Bruce Wilkinson (2001) argues that God has an incredible plan to keep us experiencing abundance in the physical, emotional, and spiritual realms of our lives. God desires that we prosper and be in health to bless others.

Pathways to God's blessings are faith to believe, connectedness with God, having a plan to bless others, and living that plan out in our lives. These prerequisites to God's blessings remind us of people like Abel, Enoch, Abraham, Mary, and Esther. Abel offered his sacrifice to God by faith. God testified of his faithfulness. Enoch walked with God, and he did not see death. He was taken up to heaven. Abraham was faithful to God, and his descendants were like the sand of the sea. Mary surrendered her mind, body, and life to God and became the mother of Jesus. Esther believed that God could deliver her and her people, and He did. Asking God to bless us indeed suggests that we know Him and believe that He will do what we ask. There is no wavering in our request. We believe that He will. Therefore, we live in anticipation of that blessing.

Let us come to God today with implicit faith in Him. He is faithful to His promises and will honor our prayers for the blessing. In the Bible, we are told that if we come to Him believing, He will grant us our request. Go to God today understanding that when we meet the prerequisite for His blessings have faith, believe, and remain connected to Him He will bless us and enlarge our territories. When God blesses us, our lives will be transformed from ordinary to extraordinary; from disgrace to grace, from devalued to valued, and from hated to blessed.

**Our Prayer for Today:** Dear God, bless me indeed and enlarge my territory. Lead me to behold You and experience Your transformation in my life. Fill me with love, joy, and peace so that I may bless others. Anoint me with oil from Your altar and fill me with grace. Give me spiritual eyesight to see the needs of others and spiritual awareness to be always cognizant of my influence on others. May I be sensitive to my influence and never hurt or injure one of Your children.

## Chapter 14
## *Experiencing God's Constancy*

God is always interceding for us. Therefore, He invites us to partner with Him in the process of transformation. We cannot transform ourselves; we can only submit to Him and allow the process to take place. There are times in our lives that we may need surgery. We submit to the anesthesiologist to put us to sleep and allow the surgeon to do his thing on us. We may be fearful, but we submit. Our lives depend on that surgery. Likewise, we need to present our hearts and entire beings to God's transforming power.

He is equal to the task. The successful doctor is competent to complete the surgery and bring healing to our physical beings.

> *We submit to the anesthesiologist to put us to sleep and allow the surgeon to do his thing on us. We may be fearful, but we submit. Our lives depend on that surgery. Likewise, we need to present our hearts and entire beings to God's transforming power.*

Similarly, we must believe that God can change our life experiences. He defeated Moab's army in the plain and delivered Israel from Haman's evil plan. He answered Daniel's prayer for forgiveness and preserved Israel's inheritance. Later, they returned to the land of their inheritance and enjoyed God's provision. There is nothing that God cannot do for you. However, you must trust His ability to deliver you and transform the situation. No problem that you encounter is too big for God to solve.

He has plans for you to prosper you and not to harm you (see Jeremiah 29:10–14). God desires that we trust Him to lead us into the future that He has prepared for us. The blessings that God wants to bestow upon you are immense. We need to ask Him to bless us, then design a plan that will allow us to be used by Him to bless others. His blessings are not meant to be hoarded, but rather to be conduits of transformation for those in need. Do not despair during challenging times. Submit to God and allow Him to do His thing in your life. The plans that He has for you cannot be changed by anyone else. He is the only one who has control over those programs. Trust Him, wait on Him and follow His directions to bring those ideas to fruition. The confirmation that the plans are genuine does not indicate that you sit idly waiting. It requires that you seek His guidance, follow His leading, and trust His plans will be realized to bless you and not harm you.

The human tendency is to panic when confronted with an impossible situation. God is saying to us that we should not panic, but rather present the case to Him. He can change the situation and honor the plans to prosper you. Isaiah reassures us that we need not fear, for we will not experience shame and disgrace (see Isaiah 54:4). God takes hold of our hands and leads us through troubled waters and intensely bad experiences (see Isaiah 43:2). The severity of the trials will not burn us to ashes, but rather build a protective shield around us for future trials. Isaiah argues further that God will help us and protect us. It is His desire and plan to answer our prayers and save us eternally. He promises to bring our children who may have strayed back to us. In Haggai 2:5, we are told that, "This is what I covenanted with you when you came out of Egypt. Moreover, my spirit remains among you. Do not fear" (NIV). Therefore, cast your fears on Him and believe that He will do what He says. God is constant and ever faithful to His promises to protect us and transform our lives so that we go forth to minister to others.

Transformation is a daily experience. It requires that we awake every morning with thanksgiving on our lips and praise in our hearts, saying "take me today and fill me, Lord. Use me in your service." Ellen White in the book *Prayer* (2002) suggests that the Savior desires us to "Consecrate ourselves to God in the morning; make this your very first work. Let your prayer be, 'Take me, O Lord, as wholly Thine. I lay my plans at Thy feet. Use me today in Thy service. Abide with me, and let all thy work be wrought in Thee.' This is a daily matter. Each morning consecrate yourself to God for that day. Surrender your plans to Him, to be carried out or given up as His providence shall indicate. Thus, day by day you may be giving your life into the hands of God, and thus, your life will be molded more and more after the life of Christ" (p. 166).

We must engage in prayer before we do anything else. Time spent with God early in the morning prepares us for meeting the trials, uncertainties, and events of our day. Our Savior spent days and nights in seasons of prayer. These prayer sessions were necessary to equip Him for the experiences of the day. He was the Savior, yet "He felt the need to experience refreshing and invigorating of the soul and body that He might meet the temptations of Satan, and those who are striving to live His life will feel this same need" (White, p. 171, 2002). As children of God who desire transformation, we need to spend quality time with God in prayer daily. At the beginning of every day, let's submit our hearts, minds, thoughts, and plans to Him and believe that the transformation will take place.

*We must engage in prayer before we do anything else.*

Claiming, believing, and living in His presence are essential prerequisites for receiving the constant flow of God's blessings. In the book *Prayer*, Ellen G. White states that "God longs to grant the requests of those who come to Him in faith. He gives to us that we may minister to others and thus become like himself" (p. 306). Therefore, it is our duty to ask with implicit confidence in God's ability and faithfulness to give to us what we ask according to His will. "Ask, and it shall be given you; seek and ye shall find; knock, and it shall be opened unto you. For everyone that asked receives; and he that seeketh findeth; and to him that knocketh it shall be opened" (Ibid).

Dear God, we thank you for Your faithfulness to us. Please take control of our minds and help us to have implicit faith in You. Help us to submit our minds and hearts to You every morning. Amen.

*Chapter 15*

# *Allowing God to Transform Your Trajectory: Connecting with His Promises*

"For I know the thoughts that I think toward you, says the Lord, thoughts of peace and not of evil, to give you a future and a hope" (Jeremiah 29:11, NKJV).

From a very young age, I knew that God had a plan for my life. I grew up in a single-parent home. My mom worked hard to ensure that we had food to eat and clothing on our bodies. She awoke at 5:00 every morning and traveled to the hotel where she was a chef. The next time she would return home would be at 11:00 p.m., sometimes even 1:00 or 2:00 a.m. She would walk along the lonely road in the dark or moonlight. I worried about her safety and would remain up until she returned home.

My mom would get ready for bed and pray this prayer every night: "Lord, give me good health, spare my life to see my daughters grow up to take care of themselves. Help me to provide for them, to educate them, to care for them. Give me good health and strength to be there for them. Open doors for me to improve their lives in this wicked world."

I knew that life was rough and rested heavily on my mother's heart. However, I knew that we were the most important people to her. We were loved and cared for, and once she was with us, everything was going to fine. There were times when life was so rough that it felt like we were the only people in the world and no one cared about us. I wondered if we were ever going to make it out of this state of poverty. What will happen to us if our mom died? What would become of my sisters and me? What would life be like when we grew up? Will we make it?

One day, I was reading my Bible and stumbled upon this text in Jeremiah 29:11. From that day, I claimed God's promise to prosper my family and me and give us hope and a future. Every day, I read the twenty-third Psalm and trusted God to be my shepherd.

My faith and trust in God grew as a result of attending the Seventh-day Adventist high school in Bequia, St. Vincent. The morning devotions, weeks of prayer, and association with godly friends transformed my life. At the age of 12, I gave my life to Jesus. It was during a week of prayer when I heard His call. My mom was happy when I told her that I wanted to be baptized. She was so happy that the next week she decided to be baptized as well. The trajectory of my family's experience was transformed.

We knew that life would be better for us now. As we grew into teens and young adults, we had to make important decisions about careers, dating, marriage, and life in general. I recalled having a conference with my sisters one Friday evening. I told them, "We are growing up into beautiful young women, and boys and men will begin looking at us. We have a choice to make. We can decide to live a godly upright life, or we could choose to become single parents and have children out of wedlock."

In my island, many individuals had children and were not married. Life for them was a constant struggle. One day I asked my sisters, "Do you see how hard our mom has to work? Do you want to live like that?"

They all responded, "No, Ella, no we are not going to live like that."

My next response to them was "Then the cycle ends right here. It must not continue with us or our children."

The next decision was 'How are we going to do that?' We outlined some plans to accomplish our big feat. We had to go to school and study to achieve our academic goals. We had to make our mom proud of us. We must get married before having babies. That meant no sex before marriage. We agreed that that was going to be our big plan. We prayed and asked God to help us carry out our plans. He did. We all completed high school, college, and university and are happily married. The legacy of living a life to the fullest must continue with total surrender to God, trusting in His will and maintaining a healthy relationship with Him. God said in His Word that He thinks positive thoughts toward us, to give us hope and a future (see Jeremiah 29:11). We must trust Him and place our futures in His hand. We must allow Him to transform/change the trajectory of our life experiences. It is imperative that we connect with His purpose for our lives. Therefore, we need to know who He is and whose we are; we must recognize our potential for greatness and live in anticipation of His transformation.

> *Living in preparation for change beckons us to develop a relationship with God, keep our goals in focus, link our purpose with God's purpose for our lives, and recognize that God thinks positive thoughts toward us.*

Living in preparation for change beckons us to develop a relationship with God, keep our goals in focus, link our purpose with God's purpose for our lives, and recognize that God thinks positive thoughts toward us. He plans to prosper us and not harm us, to give us hope and future blessings. Another important element in the process of transformation is recognizing our responsibilities to our families—parents, siblings, spouse, and children. Everyone is looking at us for guidance and light along the path to success. Every day we must surrender our lives, goals, and plans to Jesus. He is the only one who could change our situations from bad to good, from dark to bright, and from difficult to smooth.

This next section of the book will engage you in reading, meditating, and reflecting on God's Word. Through these exercises, you will experience the blessing of reading, meditating, and reflecting on God's Word using different active thinking and learning approaches. This area was inspired by my love of using active teaching and learning to help my students master content.

*Chapter 16*
# *Transformation Awaits You*

## Reading Your Way to a Transformed Life: A Daily Experience with God Rejoicing in His Presence

**Text**: "Honor and majesty are before Him; strength and gladness are in His place" (1 Chronicles 16:27, NKJV).

- *Read* the text.
- *Think* about what you have just read.
- *Meditate* on the words and message of the text.
- What is God saying to you in this text?
- I hear God saying:

_____

_____

# Chapter 16 Transformation Awaits You

_____
_____
_____
_____
_____
_____
_____
_____
_____
_____
_____
_____
_____
_____

Write the message that you just received from God on the following lines:

_____
_____
_____
_____
_____
_____
_____
_____
_____
_____
_____
_____
_____
_____

Pray the text back to God.

*Almighty Father, all glory and majesty belong to You, and power is in your hands. Father, please fill my life with joy as you fill Your temple.*

Engage in a three-to-five-minute meditation if you are at home. However, in a church or retreat setting, two to three minutes will work. Meditate and reflect on what God said to you during the prayer.

Create a concept map to illustrate the experience that you have just had.

## 56 When God Turns Our Mourning into Joy

Sing a song that matches the message that you have just received from God. Alternatively, you may listen to pre-recorded music, a CD, or DVD of the song that matches what God is saying to you.

Hymn #73 *(Seventh-day Adventist Hymnal)—Holy, Holy, Holy*

**Text**: "Give to the Lord, O families of the peoples, Give to the Lord glory and strength" (1 Chronicles 16:28, NKJV).

- *Read* the text.
- *Think* about what you have just read.
- *Meditate* on the words and message of the text.
- What is God saying to you in this text?
- I hear God saying:

_____
_____
_____
_____
_____
_____
_____
_____
_____
_____
_____
_____

How will your life be different when you give glory to the Lord?

Draw a picture to illustrate the transformation that you will experience after giving glory to God.

Write the message that you heard God saying to you.

I hear God saying to me that when I praise Him, my life will be filled with joy, happiness, and good health.

_____
_____

## Chapter 16 Transformation Awaits You

_____
_____
_____
_____
_____
_____
_____
_____
_____
_____
_____

Pray the text back to God.

*Almighty Father, I praise You, for You are worthy to be praised. I praise You for Your goodness towards me. I praise You for Your love that fills my life every day.*

Engage in a three-to-five-minute meditation if you are at home. However, in a church or retreat setting, engage in a two-to-three-minute meditation and listen to God speaking to you.

Sing a song that matches the message that you have just received from God. Alternatively, you may listen to pre-recorded music, a CD, or DVD of the song that matches what God is saying to you.

Hymn #249 (*Seventh-day Adventist Hymnal*)—*Praise Him, Praise Him!*

**Text**: "O give thanks unto the Lord; for he is good; for his mercy endureth for ever" (1 Chronicles 16:34).

- *Read* the text.
- *Think* about what you have just read.
- *Meditate* on the words and message of the text.
- What is God saying to you in this text?
- I hear God saying:

_____
_____
_____

_____
_____
_____
_____
_____
_____
_____
_____
_____

Pray the text back to God.

*Dear God, I thank You for Your marvelous eternal love. You are worthy to be loved. I love You, Lord. Help me to love myself and others with the same love I have for You.*

Engage in a three-to-five-minute meditation if you are at home. However, in a church or retreat setting, two to three minutes will work.

Write one word that summarizes your experience with God right now. Why did you choose that word to summarize your experience?

Sing a song that matches the message that you have just received from God. Alternatively, you may listen to pre-recorded music, a CD, or DVD of the song that matches what God is saying to you.

Song: *I Love You, Lord!*

**Text**: "You will show me the path of life; in your presence is the fullness of joy; at your right hand are pleasures forevermore" (Psalm 16:11, NKJV).

- *Read* the text.
- *Think* about what you have just read.
- *Meditate* on the words and message of the text.
- What is God saying to you in this text?
- I hear God saying:

_____
_____
_____

## Chapter 16 Transformation Awaits You

_____

Sing the verse back to God to express your experience in His presence.

Pray the text back to God.

*Father, help me to experience life that is filled with joy. Show me the path on which I need to walk and help me to experiences pleasure forevermore.*

Write your prayer on the lines below.

_____

Engage in a three-to-five-minute meditation if you are at home. However, in a church or retreat setting, a two-to-three-minute meditation will work. Listen to God speaking to you.

Sing a song that matches the message that you have just received from God. Alternatively, you may listen to pre-recorded music, a CD, or DVD of the song that matches what God is saying to you.

Hymn: #619 (*Seventh-day Adventist Hymnal*)—*Lead On, O King Eternal*

# 60   When God Turns Our Mourning into Joy

**Text**: "Behold, the maidservant of the Lord! Let it be to me according to your word" (Luke 1:38, NKJV).

- *Read* the text.
- *Think* about what you have just read.
- *Meditate* on the words and message of the text.
- What is God saying to you in this text?
- I hear God saying:

_____
_____
_____
_____
_____
_____
_____
_____
_____
_____
_____

Pray the text back to God.

Engage in a three-to-five-minute meditation if you are at home. However, in a church or retreat setting, a two-to-three-minute meditation will work. Listen to God speaking to you.

Write a one-sentence summary to explain what you've just experienced in the presence of God.

_____
_____
_____
_____
_____
_____

## Chapter 16 Transformation Awaits You 61

_____
_____
_____
_____

Sing a song that matches the message that you have just received from God. Alternatively, you may listen to pre-recorded music, a CD, or DVD of the song that matches what God is saying to you.

Hymn: #309 (*Seventh-day Adventist Hymnal*)—*I Surrender All*

**Text**: "You will show me the path that leads to life. Your presence fills me with joy and brings the pleasure forever" (Psalm 16:11, GNT).

- *Read* the text.
- *Think* about what you have just read.
- *Meditate* on the words and message of the text.
- What is God saying to you in this text?
- I hear God saying:

_____
_____
_____
_____
_____
_____
_____
_____
_____
_____
_____

Pray the text back to God.

Engage in a three-to-five-minute meditation if you are at home. However, in a church or retreat setting, two-to-three minute meditation will work. Listen to God speaking to you.

Kindly identify a text with a similar message that is speaking to your heart right now.

Write the text here.

_____
_____
_____
_____
_____
_____
_____
_____
_____
_____
_____
_____

Sing a song that matches the message that you have just received from God. Alternatively, you may listen to pre-recorded music, a CD, or DVD of the song that matches what God is saying to you.

Hymn: #529 (*Seventh-day Adventist Hymnal*)—*Under His Wings*

**Texts**: "Praise the Lord, all people on earth, praise His glory and might." (Psalm 96:7, GNT).

"Praise the Lord, because you have saved me and kept my enemies from gloating over me" (Psalm 30:1, GNT).

- *Read* the text.
- *Think* about what you have just read.
- *Meditate* on the words and message of the text.
- What is God saying to you in this text?
- I hear God saying:

_____
_____

## Chapter 16  Transformation Awaits You

Engage in a 3 to 5 mins meditation if you are at home. However, in a church or retreat setting, 2 to 3 minutes meditation will work. Listen to God speaking to you.

What was the most important thing that you learned while in God's presence today?

Sing a song that matches the message that you have just received from God. Alternatively, you may listen to pre-recorded music, a CD, or DVD of the song that matches what God is saying to you.

Hymn: #590 (*Seventh-day Adventist Hymnal*)—*Trust and Obey*

**Text**: "And He said, My presence will go with you, and I will give you rest" (Exodus 33:14, NKJV).

- *Read* the text.
- *Think* about what you have just read.
- *Meditate* on the words and message of the text.
- What is God saying to you in this text?
- I hear God saying:

# 64  When God Turns Our Mourning into Joy

_____
_____
_____
_____
_____
_____

Pray the text back to God.

Engage in a three-to-five-minute meditation if you are at home. However, in a church or retreat setting, two-to-three minute meditation will work. Listen to God speaking to you.

Write a one-sentence summary of your self-perceptions after reading, listening to God, and meditating on His words.

Sing a song that matches the message that you have just received from God. Alternatively, you may listen to pre-recorded music, a CD, or DVD of the song that matches what God is saying to you.

**Text**: "And Mary said: my soul magnifies the Lord, and my spirit has rejoiced in God my Savior" (Luke 1:46–47, NKJV).

- *Read* the text.
- *Think* about what you have just read.
- *Meditate* on the words and message of the text.
- What is God saying to you in this text?
- I hear God saying:

_____
_____
_____
_____
_____
_____
_____
_____
_____

## Chapter 16 Transformation Awaits You

_____
_____

Pray the text back to God.

Engage in a three-to-five-minute meditation if you are at home. However, in a church or retreat setting, two to three minutes will work. Meditate and listen to God speaking to you.

How do you feel about yourself after you read the text, listened to God speaking to you, and meditated on His word?

What are three adjustments that you will make in your thinking now?

1.

2.

3.

Sing a song that matches the message that you have just received from God. Alternatively, you may listen to pre-recorded music, a CD, or DVD of the song that matches what God is saying to you.

**Text**: "Honour and majesty are before him: strength and beauty are in his sanctuary" (Psalm 96:6).

- *Read* the text.
- *Think* about what you have just read.
- *Meditate* on the words and message of the text.
- What is God saying to you in this text?
- I hear God saying:

_____
_____
_____
_____
_____
_____
_____

Pray the text back to God.

Engage in a three-to-five-minute meditation if you are at home. However, in a church or retreat setting, two to three minutes meditation will work. Listen to God speaking to you.

What misconceptions did you have about God before reading the text, meditating on God's words, and listening to him?

How have your misconceptions changed since your experience with God today?

## Chapter 16 Transformation Awaits You

_____
_____
_____

Sing a song that matches the message that you have just received from God. Alternatively, you may listen to pre-recorded music, a CD, or DVD of the song that matches what God is saying to you.

**Hymn:** #270 (*Seventh-day Adventist Hymnal*)—*O Holy Dove of God Descending*

**Text:** "Clap your hands, all you nations; shout to God with cries of joy. For the Lord Most High is awesome, the great King over all the earth. He subdued nations under us, peoples under our feet" (Psalm 47:1–3, NIV).

- *Read* the text.
- *Think* about what you have just read.
- *Meditate* on the words and message of the text.
- What is God saying to you in this text?
- I hear God saying:

_____
_____
_____
_____
_____
_____
_____
_____
_____
_____
_____

Pray the text back to God.

Engage in a three-to-five-minute meditation if you are at home. However, in a church or retreat setting, two to three minutes will work. Meditate and listen to God speaking to you.

## 68   When God Turns Our Mourning into Joy

Reflect on the concept of the *awesomeness of God*; then list several ideas that come to mind that are closely related to the *awesomeness of God*.

Sing a song that matches the message that you have just received from God. Alternatively, you may listen to pre-recorded music, a CD, or DVD of the song that matches what God is saying to you.

**Hymn:** #12 (*Seventh-day Adventist Hymnal*)—*Joyful, Joyful, We Adore Thee*

**Text**: "My lips shall greatly rejoice when I sing to You. And my soul, which You have redeemed" (Psalm 71:23, NKJV).

- *Read* the text.
- *Think* about what you have just read.
- *Meditate* on the words and message of the text.
- What is God saying to you in this text?
- I hear God saying:

_____
_____
_____
_____
_____
_____
_____
_____
_____
_____
_____

Pray the text back to God.

Engage in a three-to-five-minute meditation if you are at home. However, in a church or retreat setting, two to three minutes will work. Meditate and listen to God speaking to you.

## Chapter 16 Transformation Awaits You

Draw or paint a picture to illustrate what you feel after reading the text, meditating on His words, and listening to Him.

How do you feel right now?

Sing a song that matches the message that you have just received from God. Alternatively, you may listen to pre-recorded music, a CD, or DVD of the song that matches what God is saying to you.

Hymn: #27 (*Seventh-day Adventist Hymnal*)—*Rejoice, Ye Pure in Heart!*

**Text:** "My tongue also shall talk to Your righteousness all the day long; For they are confounded, for they are brought to shame who seek my hurt" (Psalm 71:24, NKJV)

- *Read* the text.
- *Think* about what you have just read.
- *Meditate* on the words and message of the text.
- What is God saying to you in this text?
- I hear God saying:

_____
_____
_____
_____
_____
_____
_____
_____
_____
_____
_____
_____

Pray the text back to God.

Engage in a three-to-five-minute meditation if you are at home. However, in a church or retreat setting, two to three minutes will work. Meditate and listen to God speaking to you.

## 70  When God Turns Our Mourning into Joy

How do you think speaking of God's righteousness all day long will impact on your mental and emotional health?

_____
_____
_____
_____
_____
_____
_____
_____
_____
_____
_____
_____

Sing song that matches the message that you have just received from God. Alternatively, you may listen to pre-recorded music, a CD, or DVD of the song that matches what God is saying to you.

Hymn: #242 (*Seventh-day Adventist Hymnal*)—*Jesus, Thou Joy of Loving Hearts*

*Chapter 17*

# *Experiencing His Peace*

**Text**: "And she was in bitterness of soul, and prayed unto the LORD, and wept sore. And she vowed a vow, and said, O LORD of hosts, if thou wilt indeed look on the affliction of thine handmaid, and remember me, and not forget thine handmaid, but wilt give unto thine handmaid a man child, then I will give him unto the LORD all the days of his life" (1 Samuel 1:10–11).

- *Read* the text.
- *Think* about what you have just read.
- *Meditate* on the words and message of the text.
- What is God saying to you in this text?
- I hear God saying:

_____
_____
_____
_____

## 72   When God Turns Our Mourning into Joy

Pray the text back to God.

Engage in a three-to-five-minute meditation if you are at home. However, in a church or retreat setting, two to three minutes will work. Meditate and listen to God speaking to you.

How do you envision your experience with God will change after praying to God passionately?

Sing a song that matches the message that you have just received from God. Or you may listen to pre-recorded music, a CD, or DVD of the song that matches what God is saying to you.

Hymn: #466 (*Seventh-day Adventist Hymnal*)—*Wonderful Peace*

**Text**: "For I know the thoughts I think towards you, says the Lord, thoughts of peace and not of evil, to give you a future and a hope" (Jeremiah 29:11, NKJV).

- *Read* the text.

Chapter 17 Experiencing His Peace 73

- *Think* about what you have just read.
- *Meditate* on the words and message of the text.
- What is God saying to you in this text?
- I hear God saying:

_____
_____
_____
_____
_____
_____
_____
_____
_____
_____
_____
_____

Pray the text back to God.

Engage in a three-to-five-minute meditation if you are at home. However, in a church or retreat setting, two to three minutes will work. Meditate and listen to God speaking to you.

How do you think your life will change as a result of believing this text and claiming it in your life? List three ways in which your life will be different as a result of embracing this text.

1.

2.

3.

Sing a song that matches the message that you have just received from God. Alternatively, you may listen to pre-recorded music, a CD, or DVD of the song that matches what God is saying to you.

Hymn: #532 (*Seventh-day Adventist Hymnal*)—*Day by Day*

**Text**: "Be anxious for nothing, but in everything by prayer and supplication, with thanksgiving, let your requests be made known to God; and the

# 74   When God Turns Our Mourning into Joy

peace of God, which surpasses all understanding, will guard your hearts and minds through Christ Jesus'"" (Philippians 4:6, NKJV)

- *Read* the text.
- *Think* about what you have just read.
- *Meditate* on the words and message of the text.
- What is God saying to you in this text?
- I hear God saying:

_____
_____
_____
_____
_____
_____
_____
_____
_____
_____

Pray the text back to God.

Engage in a three-to-five-minute meditation if you are at home. However, in a church or retreat setting, two to three minutes will work. Meditate and listen to God speaking to you.

What is the "Big Idea" in today's devotional texts?

Write three details that support this "Big Idea."

1.

2.

3.

# Chapter 17 Experiencing His Peace

Sing a song that matches the message that you have just received from God. Alternatively, you may listen to pre-recorded music, a CD, or DVD of the song that matches what God is saying to you.

**Hymn:** #524 (*Seventh-day Adventist Hymnal*)—*'Tis So Sweet to Trust in Jesus*

**Text:** "And I say unto you, Ask, and it shall be given you; seek, and ye shall find; knock, and it shall be opened unto you. For every one that asketh receiveth; and he that seeketh findeth; and to him that knocketh it shall be opened. If a son shall ask bread of any of you that is a father, will he give him a stone? or if he ask a fish, will he for a fish give him a serpent? Or if he shall ask an egg, will he offer him a scorpion? If ye then, being evil, know how to give good gifts unto your children: how much more shall your heavenly Father give the Holy Spirit to them that ask him'" (Luke 11:9–13)?

- *Read* the text.
- *Think* about what you have just read.
- *Meditate* on the words and message of the text.
- What is God saying to you in this text?
- I hear God saying:

_____
_____
_____
_____
_____
_____
_____
_____
_____
_____
_____

Pray the text back to God.

## 76  When God Turns Our Mourning into Joy

Engage in a three-to-five-minute meditation if you are at home. However, in a church or retreat setting, two to three minutes will work. Meditate and listen to God speaking to you.

What change in your daily life will you make as a result of reading the texts, meditating on God's words, and listening to Him today?

Sing a song that matches the message that you have just received from God. Or you may listen to pre-recorded music, a CD, or DVD of the song that matches what God is saying to you.

Hymn: #224 *(Seventh-day Adventist Hymnal)*—*Seek Ye First the Kingdom*

Hymn: #539 *(Seventh-day Adventist Hymnal)*—*I Will Early Seek the Savior*

**Text:** "And coming at that instant she gave thanks to the Lord, and spoke of Him to all those who looked for redemption in Jerusalem" (Luke 2:38, NKJV).

- *Read* the text.
- *Think* about what you have just read.
- *Meditate* on the words and message of the text.
- What is God saying to you in this text?
- I hear God saying:

_____
_____
_____
_____
_____
_____
_____
_____
_____
_____
_____

Pray the text back to God.

# Chapter 17 Experiencing His Peace

Engage in a three-to-five-minute meditation if you are at home. However, in a church or retreat setting, two to three minutes will work. Meditate and listen to God speaking to you.

How would life be different as a result of what you just heard God saying to you?

_____
_____
_____
_____
_____
_____
_____
_____
_____
_____
_____
_____
_____

Sing a song that matches the message that you have just received from God. Or you may listen to pre-recorded music, a CD, or DVD of the song that matches what God is saying to you.

Hymn: #249 (*Seventh-day Adventist Hymnal*)—*Praise Him! Praise Him!*

**Text**: "And this woman was a widow of about eighty-four years, who did not depart from the temple, but served God with fasting and prayers night and day" (Luke 2:37, NKJV).

- *Read* the text.
- *Think* about what you have just read.
- *Meditate* on the words and message of the text.
- What is God saying to you in this text?
- I hear God saying:

_____
_____
_____
_____

78   When God Turns Our Mourning into Joy

_____
_____
_____
_____
_____
_____
_____

Pray the text back to God.

Engage in a three-to-five-minute meditation if you are at home. However, in a church or retreat setting, two to three minutes will work.

What important lesson did you learn about how to live in this world from Anna's experience?

_____
_____
_____
_____
_____
_____
_____
_____
_____
_____
_____

Sing a song that matches the message that you have just received from God. Or you may listen to pre-recorded music, a CD, or DVD of the song that matches what God is saying to you.

Hymn: #694 (*Seventh-day Adventist Hymnal*)—*Praise God, From Whom All Blessings*

**Text**: "Hannah spoke in her heart; only her lips moved, but her voice was not heard" (1 Samuel 1:13, NKJV).

- *Read* the text.
- *Think* about what you have just read.

# Chapter 17 Experiencing His Peace

- *Meditate* on the words and message of the text.
- What is God saying to you in this text?
- I hear God saying:

_____
_____
_____
_____
_____
_____
_____
_____
_____
_____
_____
_____

Present the burden of your heart to God.

Engage in a three-to-five-minute meditation if you are at home. However, in a church or retreat setting, two to three minutes will work. Meditate and listen to God speaking to you.

What does praying to God in the quietude of your soul do to enhance your relationship with Him and help you to experience peace?

_____
_____
_____
_____
_____
_____
_____
_____
_____
_____
_____

80  When God Turns Our Mourning into Joy

Sing a song that matches the message that you have just received from God. Or you may listen to pre-recorded music, a CD, or DVD of the song that matches what God is saying to you.

Hymn: #305 (*Seventh-day Adventist Hymnal*)—Give Me Jesus

**Text**: "And Hezekiah received the letter from the hand of the messengers, and read it: and Hezekiah went up unto the house of the Lord, and spread it before the Lord" (Isaiah 37:14).

- *Read* the text.
- *Think* about what you have just read.
- *Meditate* on the words and message of the text.
- What is God saying to you in this text?
- I hear God saying:

_____
_____
_____
_____
_____
_____
_____
_____
_____
_____
_____

Do you have a prayer challenge? Spread it before God right now.

Engage in a three-to-five-minute meditation if you are at home. However, in a church or retreat setting, two to three minutes will work. Meditate and listen to God speaking to you.

## Chapter 17 Experiencing His Peace

Write a one-paragraph summary of how you will handle a prayer challenge from this day forward.

_____
_____
_____
_____
_____
_____
_____
_____
_____

Sing a song that matches the message that you have just received from God. Or you may listen to pre-recorded music, a CD, or DVD of the song that matches what God is saying to you.

Hymn: #532 (*Seventh-day Adventist Hymnal*)—*Day by Day*

Do you have a prayer challenge? Spread it to God right now.

**Text**: "Now therefore, O Lord our God, save us from his hand, that all the kingdoms of the earth may know that thou art the Lord, even thou only" (Isaiah 37:20).

- *Read* the text.
- *Think* about what you have just read.
- *Meditate* on the words and message of the text.
- What is God saying to you in this text?
- I hear God saying:

_____
_____
_____
_____
_____
_____
_____

## 82   When God Turns Our Mourning into Joy

_____
_____
_____

Pray the text back to God.

Engage in a three-to-five-minute meditation if you are at home. However, in a church or retreat setting, two to three minutes will work. Meditate and listen to God speaking to you.

_____
_____
_____
_____
_____
_____
_____
_____
_____
_____

Sing a song that matches the message that you have just received from God. Or you may listen to pre-recorded music, a CD, or DVD of the song that matches what God is saying to you.

**Hymn**: #85 (*Seventh-day Adventist Hymnal*)—*Eternal Father, Strong to Save*

**Text**: "Incline thine ear, O Lord, and hear; open thine eyes, O Lord, and see: and hear all the words of Sennacherib, which hath sent to reproach the living God" (Isaiah 37:17).

- *Read* the text.
- *Think* about what you have just read.
- *Meditate* on the words and message of the text.
- What is God saying to you in this text?
- I hear God saying:

_____
_____
_____
_____
_____
_____
_____
_____
_____
_____
_____
_____
_____
_____
_____

Pray the text back to God.

Engage in a three-to-five-minute meditation if you are at home. However, in a church or retreat setting, two to three minutes will work. Meditate and listen to God speaking to you.

Sing a song that matches the message that you have just received from God. Or you may listen to pre-recorded music, a CD, or DVD of the song that matches what God is saying to you.

Hymn: #480 (*Seventh-day Adventist Hymnal*)—*Dear Lord and Father*

**Text**: "Now therefore, O Lord our God, save us from his hand, that all the kingdoms of the earth may know that thou art the Lord, even thou only" (Isaiah 37:20).

- *Read* the text.
- *Think* about what you have just read.
- *Meditate* on the words and message of the text.
- What is God saying to you in this text?
- I hear God saying:

_____
_____
_____
_____
_____
_____

# 84  When God Turns Our Mourning into Joy

_____
_____
_____
_____
_____
_____

Pray the text back to God.

Engage in a three-to-five-minute meditation if you are at home. However, in a church or retreat setting, two to three minutes will work. Meditate and listen to God speaking to you.

How would your life be different after Jesus saves you from your enemies, calamity, or impending doom?

_____
_____
_____
_____
_____
_____
_____
_____
_____
_____
_____
_____

Sing a song that matches the message that you have just received from God. Or you may listen to pre-recorded music, a CD, or DVD of the song that matches what God is saying to you.

Hymn: #7 (*Seventh-day Adventist Hymnal*)—*The Lord in Zion Reigneth*

**Text**: "And Jehoshaphat feared and set himself to seek the Lord, and proclaimed a fast throughout all Judah. And Judah gathered themselves together, to ask help of the Lord: even out of all the cities of Judah they came to seek the Lord" (2 Chronicles 20:3–4).

- *Read* the text.

# Chapter 17 Experiencing His Peace

- *Think* about what you have just read.
- *Meditate* on the words and message of the text.
- What is God saying to you in this text?
- I hear God saying:

_____
_____
_____
_____
_____
_____
_____
_____
_____
_____
_____
_____

Pray the text back to God.

Engage in a three-to-five-minute meditation if you are at home. However, in a church or retreat setting, two to three minutes will work. Meditate and listen to God speaking to you.

What transformation will you experience after engaging in prayer and fasting?

_____
_____
_____
_____
_____
_____
_____
_____
_____
_____
_____
_____

Sing a song that matches the message that you have just received from God. Or you may listen to pre-recorded music, a CD, or DVD of the song that matches what God is saying to you.

Hymn: #529 (*Seventh-day Adventist Hymnal*)—*Under His Wings*

**Text**: "For we have no power to face this vast army that is attacking us. We do not know what to do, but our eyes are on you" (1 Chronicles 20:12, NIV).

- *Read* the text.
- *Think* about what you have just read.
- *Meditate* on the words and message of the text.
- What is God saying to you in this text?
- I hear God saying:

_____
_____
_____
_____
_____
_____
_____
_____
_____
_____
_____
_____

Pray the text back to God.

Engage in a three-to-five-minute meditation if you are at home. However, in a church or retreat setting, two to three minutes will work. Meditate and listen to God speaking to you.

Write a one-sentence summary of how you visualize your life will change as a result of living this text and praying this prayer.

## Chapter 17 Experiencing His Peace

_____
_____
_____
_____
_____
_____
_____
_____
_____
_____
_____
_____

Sing a song that matches the message that you have just received from God. Or you may listen to pre-recorded music, a CD, or DVD of the song that matches what God is saying to you.

Hymn: #535 (*Seventh-day Adventist Hymnal*)—*I Am Trusting Thee, Lord Jesus*

**Text**: "O God, thou art my God; early will I seek thee: my soul thirsteth for thee, my flesh longeth for thee in a dry and thirsty land, where no water is" (Psalm 63:1).

- *Read* the text.
- *Think* about what you have just read.
- *Meditate* on the words and message of the text.
- What is God saying to you in this text?
- I hear God saying:

_____
_____
_____
_____
_____
_____
_____
_____

_____
_____

Pray the text back to God.

Engage in a three-to-five-minute meditation if you are at home. However, in a church or retreat setting, two to three minutes will work.

Create two lists to illustrate the change that you will experience as a result of seeking God early in the morning.

Before:

After:

Sing a song that matches the message that you have just received from God. Alternatively, you may listen to pre-recorded music, a CD, or DVD of the song that matches what God is saying to you.

Song: *As the Deer*

**Text**: "No weapon that is formed against thee shall prosper; and every tongue that shall rise against thee in judgment thou shalt condemn. This is the heritage of the servants of the Lord, and their righteousness is of me, saith the Lord" (Isaiah 54: 17).

- *Read* the text.
- *Think* about what you have just read.
- *Meditate* on the words and message of the text.
- What is God saying to you in this text?
- I hear God saying:

_____
_____
_____
_____
_____
_____
_____
_____

# Chapter 17  Experiencing His Peace

_____
_____
_____

Pray the text back to God.

Engage in a three-to-five-minute meditation if you are at home. However, in a church or retreat setting, two to three minutes will work. Meditate and listen to God speaking to you.

Draw a picture to illustrate what your life will be like after allowing God to destroy every weapon and condemn every tongue that is targeting you.

Sing a song that matches the message that you have just received from God. Or you may listen to pre-recorded music, a CD, or DVD of the song that matches what God is saying to you.

Hymn: #412 (*Seventh-day Adventist Hymnal*)—*Cover With His Life*

Text: "For we have no power against this great multitude that is coming against us; nor do we know what to do, but our eyes are upon you" (2 Chronicles 20:12, NKJV).

- *Read* the text.
- *Think* about what you have just read.
- *Meditate* on the words and message of the text.
- What is God saying to you in this text?
- I hear God saying:

_____
_____
_____
_____
_____
_____
_____
_____
_____

## When God Turns Our Mourning into Joy

Pray the text back to God.

Engage in a three-to-five-minute meditation if you are at home. However, in a church or retreat setting, two to three minutes will work. Meditate and listen to God speaking to you.

Write a paragraph to explain how your life will be transformed as a result of keeping your eyes on Jesus.

_____
_____
_____
_____
_____
_____
_____
_____
_____
_____
_____
_____

Sing a song that matches the message that you have just received from God. Or you may listen to pre-recorded music, a CD, or DVD of the song that matches what God is saying to you.

**Hymn**: #88 (*Seventh-day Adventist Hymnal*)—*I Sing the Mighty Power of God*

**Text**: "Hear my cry, O God; attend to my prayer. From the end of the earth I will cry to you, when my heart is overwhelmed; lead me to the rock that is higher than I. For you have been a shelter for me" (Psalm 61:1–3, NKJV).

- *Read* the text twice. The first time just read it through, the second time, read it slowly, identifying the key words and reflect on what God is saying to you.
- *Think* about what you have just read.
- *Meditate* on the words and message of the text.
- What is God saying to you in this text?

Chapter 17 Experiencing His Peace 91

- I hear God saying:

_____
_____
_____
_____
_____
_____
_____
_____
_____
_____
_____
_____
_____

Sing songs that reflect what God is saying to you.

Hymn: #36 (*Seventh-day Adventist Hymnal*)—*O Thou in Whose Presence*

Hymn: #525 (*Seventh-day Adventist Hymnal*)—*Hiding in Thee*

Draw a picture that illustrates what God has just done for you.

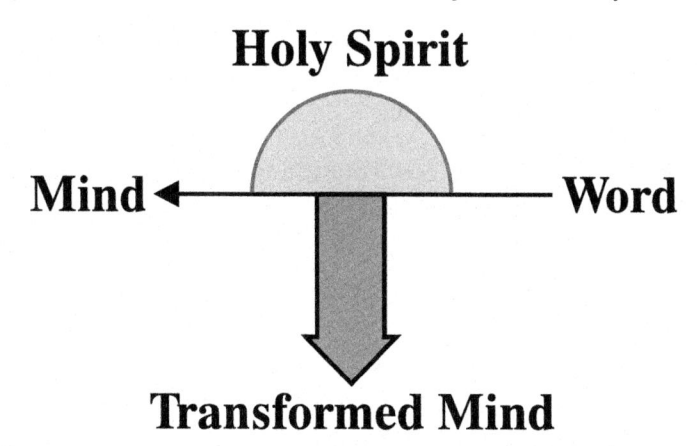

# Holy Spirit

**Mind** ← — **Word**

↓

# Transformed Mind

**Text**: "Then I will sprinkle clean water on you, and you shall be clean; I will cleanse you from all your filthiness and all your idols. I will give you a new heart and put a new spirit within you; I will take the heart of stone out of your flesh and give you a heart of flesh. I will put my spirit with-in you and cause you to walk in my statutes, and you will keep my judgments and do them" (Ezekiel 36:25–27, NKJV).

- *Read* the text.

## 92  When God Turns Our Mourning into Joy

- *Think* about what you have just read.
- *Meditate* on the words and message of the text.
- What is God saying to you in this text?
- I hear God saying:

_____
_____
_____
_____
_____
_____
_____
_____
_____
_____
_____

Pray the text back to God.

Engage in a three-to-five-minute meditation if you are at home. However, in a church or retreat setting, two to three minutes will work. Meditate and listen to God speaking to you.

Write three words to express how your life will change as a result of God pouring the cleansing power of the Holy Spirit over you.

1.

2.

3.

Sing a song that matches the message that you have just received from God. Or you may listen to pre-recorded music, a CD, or DVD of the song that matches what God is saying to you.

Hymn: #332 (*Seventh-day Adventist Hymnal*)—*The Cleansing Wave*

**Text**: "Ah Lord God! behold, thou hast made the heaven and the earth by thy great power and stretched out arm, and there is nothing too hard for thee... Behold, I am the Lord, the God of all flesh: is there any thing too hard for me" (Jeremiah 32:17, 27)?

- *Read* the text.
- *Think* about what you have just read.
- *Meditate* on the words and message of the text.
- What is God saying to you in this text?
- I hear God saying:

_____

Pray the text back to God.

Engage in a three-to-five-minute meditation if you are at home. However, in a church or retreat setting, two to three minutes will work. Listen to God speaking to you.

How do you feel after you recognize that there is nothing too hard for God to do?

_____

Sing a song that matches the message that you have just received from God. Or you may listen to pre-recorded music, a CD, or DVD of the song that matches what God is saying to you.

Hymn: #253 (*Seventh-day Adventist Hymnal*)—There's No Other Name Like Jesus

Hymn: #294 (*Seventh-day Adventist Hymnal*)—Power in the Blood.

**Text**: "Call unto me, and I will answer thee, and show thee great and mighty things, which thou knowest not" (Jeremiah 33:3).

- *Read* the text.
- *Think* about what you have just read.
- *Meditate* on the words and message of the text.
- What is God saying to you in this text?
- I hear God saying:

_____
_____
_____
_____
_____
_____
_____
_____
_____
_____

Pray the text back to God.

Engage in a three-to-five-minute meditation if you are at home. However, in a church or retreat setting, two to three minutes will work. Listen to God speaking to you.

What is the one word of the text that summarizes the power of the text? How will your life change as a result of this keyword that you just identified?

_____
_____
_____
_____
_____
_____
_____
_____
_____
_____
_____
_____

Sing a song that matches the message that you have just received from God. Or you may listen to pre-recorded music, a CD, or DVD of the song that matches what God is saying to you.

Hymn: #282 (*Seventh-day Adventist Hymnal*)—*I Hear Thy Welcome Voice*

*Chapter 18*
# God's Faithfulness

**Text**: "For with God nothing shall be impossible. And Mary said, Behold the handmaid of the Lord; be it unto me according to thy word" (Luke 1:37–38).

- *Read* the text.
- *Think* about what you have just read.
- *Meditate* on the words and message of the text.
- What is God saying to you in this text?
- I hear God saying:

_____
_____
_____
_____
_____
_____

Pray the text back to God.

Engage in a three-to-five-minute meditation if you are at home. However, in a church or retreat setting, two to three minutes will work. Meditate and listen to God speaking to you.

How would your response to challenges in your life be different as a result of living in the reality of this text?

Sing a song that matches the message that you have just received from God. Or you may listen to pre-recorded music, a CD, or DVD of the song that matches what God is saying to you.

Hymn: #524 (*Seventh-day Adventist Hymnal*)—*'Tis So Sweet to Trust in Jesus*

**Text**: "The Lord is my strength and song, and he is become my salvation: he is my God, and I will prepare him an habitation; my father's God, and I will exalt him" (Exodus 15:2).

- *Read* the text
- *Think* about what you have just read.

- *Meditate* on the words and message of the text.
- What is God saying to you in this text?
- I hear God saying:

___

Pray the text back to God.

Engage in a three-to-five-minute meditation if you are at home. However, in a church or retreat setting, two to three minutes will work. Meditate and listen to God speaking to you.

What changes would you experience when you praise, exalt, and allow God to be your strength and salvation?

___

Sing a song that matches the message that you have just received from God. Or you may listen to pre-recorded music, a CD, or DVD of the song that matches what God is saying to you.

Hymn: #4 (*Seventh-day Adventist Hymnal*)—*Praise, my Soul, the King of Heaven*

**Text**: "Wait on the Lord; be of good courage, and He shall strengthen your heart; wait, I say, on the Lord" (Psalm 27:14).

- *Read* the text
- *Think* about what you have just read.
- *Meditate* on the words and message of the text.
- What is God saying to you in this text?
- I hear God saying:

_____
_____
_____
_____
_____
_____
_____
_____
_____
_____
_____
_____
_____

Pray the text back to God.

Engage in a three-to-five-minute meditation if you are at home. However, in a church or retreat setting, two to three minutes will work. Meditate and listen to God speaking to you.

Identify three benefits that you will experience as a result of waiting on the Lord.

1. _____

## When God Turns Our Mourning into Joy

2. _____

3. _____

Draw a picture to illustrate your feelings after experiencing the three benefits that you identified.

Sing a song that matches the message that you have just received from God. Or you may listen to pre-recorded music, a CD, or DVD of the song that matches what God is saying to you.

Hymn: #7 (*Seventh-day Adventist Hymnal*)—*The Lord in Zion Reigneth*

**Text:**, "But I will hope continually, and will yet praise thee more and more" (Psalm 71:14).

- *Read* the text
- *Think* about what you have just read.
- *Meditate* on the words and message of the text.
- What is God saying to you in this text?
- I hear God saying:

_____
_____
_____
_____
_____
_____
_____
_____
_____
_____

Pray the text back to God.

Engage in a three-to-five-minute meditation if you are at home. However, in a church or retreat setting, two to three minutes will work. Meditate and listen to God speaking to you.

Chapter 18 God's Faithfulness 101

What transformation in your attitude will you experience when you make this text a part of your life?

_____
_____
_____
_____
_____
_____
_____
_____
_____
_____
_____
_____
_____

Sing a song that matches the message that you have just received from God. Or you may listen to pre-recorded music, a CD, or DVD of the song that matches what God is saying to you.

Hymn: #522 (*Seventh-day Adventist Hymnal*)—*My Hope is Built on Nothing Less*

**Text:** " Fear thou not; for I am with thee: be not dismayed; for I am thy God: I will strengthen thee; yea, I will help thee; yea, I will uphold thee with the right hand of my" (Isaiah 41:10).

- *Read* the text
- *Think* about what you have just read.
- *Meditate* on the words and message of the text.
- What is God saying to you in this text?
- I hear God saying:

_____
_____
_____
_____
_____
_____

_____
_____
_____
_____
_____
_____

Pray the text back to God.

Engage in a three-to-five-minute meditation if you are at home. However, in a church or retreat setting, two to three minutes will work. Meditate and listen to God speaking to you.

Draw a picture to illustrate what your life will be when you experience the promises in this text.

Sing a song that matches the message that you have just received from God. Or you may listen to pre-recorded music, a CD, or DVD of the song that matches what God is saying to you.

Hymn: #532 (*Seventh-day Adventist Hymnal*)—*Day by Day*

**Text**: "These things I have spoken to you, that in Me you may have peace. In the world you will have tribulation; but be of good cheer, I have overcome the world" (John 16:33, NKJV).

- *Read* the text
- *Think* about what you have just read.
- *Meditate* on the words and message of the text.
- What is God saying to you in this text?
- I hear God saying:

_____
_____
_____
_____
_____
_____
_____
_____

## Chapter 18 God's Faithfulness 103

_____
_____
_____
_____

Pray the text back to God.

Engage in a three-to-five-minute meditation if you are at home. However, in a church or retreat setting, two to three minutes will work. Listen to God speaking to you.

Create a picture to illustrate the peace that you will experience after you've turned your situation over to God.

Sing a song that matches the message that you have just received from God. Or you may listen to pre-recorded music, a CD, or DVD of the song that matches what God is saying to you.

Hymn: #466 (*Seventh-day Adventist Hymnal*)—*Wonderful Peace*

**Text:** "Then Peter said to them, Repent, and let every one of you be baptized in the name of Jesus Christ for the remission of sins; and you shall receive the gift of the Holy Spirit" (Acts 2:38, NKJV).

- *Read* the text

- *Think* about what you have just read.

- *Meditate* on the words and message of the text.

- What is God saying to you in this text?

- I hear God saying:

_____
_____
_____
_____
_____
_____
_____
_____
_____
_____

Pray the text back to God.

Engage in a three-to-five-minute meditation if you are at home. However, in a church or retreat setting, two to three minutes will work. Listen to God speaking to you.

For the next minute, write the impact of repentance, baptism, and receipt of the Holy Spirit in your life.

Sing a song that matches the message that you have just received from God. Alternatively, you may listen to pre-recorded music, a CD, or DVD of the song that matches what God is saying to you.

Hymn: #258 (*Seventh-day Adventist Hymnal*)—*Baptize Us Anew*

**Text**: "There is no fear in love; but perfect love casteth out fear: because fear hath torment. He that feareth is not made perfect in love" (1 John 4:18).

- *Read* the text
- *Think* about what you have just read.
- *Meditate* on the words and message of the text.
- What is God saying to you in this text?
- I hear God saying:

Chapter 18 God's Faithfulness 105

Pray the text back to God.

Engage in a three-to-five-minute meditation if you are at home. However, in a church or retreat setting, two to three minutes will work. Meditate and listen to God speaking to you.

How would your life be different after you have experienced the perfect love of God? Think and either write or draw your response.

_____
_____
_____
_____
_____
_____
_____
_____
_____
_____
_____

Sing a song that matches the message that you have just received from God. Or you may listen to pre-recorded music, a CD, or DVD of the song that matches what God is saying to you.

Hymn: #76 (*Seventh-day Adventist Hymnal*)—*O Love That Wwilt Not Llet Me Go*

**Text**: "Now David was greatly distressed, for the people spoke of stoning him, because the soul of all the people was grieved, every man for his sons and his daughters. But David strengthened himself in the Lord his God" (1 Samuel 30:6, NKJV).

- *Read* the text
- *Think* about what you have just read.
- *Meditate* on the words and message of the text.
- What is God saying to you in this text?
- I hear God saying:

Pray the text back to God.

Engage in a three-to-five-minute meditation if you are at home. However, in a church or retreat setting, two to three minutes will work. Meditate and listen to God speaking to you.

Think of a time when you were distressed. How did God strengthen you? How has your response to distress changed after this experience?

Sing a song that matches the message that you have just received from God. Or you may listen to pre-recorded music, a CD, or DVD of the song that matches what God is saying to you.

Hymn: #415 (*Seventh-day Adventist Hymnal*)—*Christ the Lord, All Power Possessing*

# Chapter 18  God's Faithfulness

**Text**: "The Lord is my light and salvation; whom shall I fear? The Lord is the strength of my life; of whom shall I be afraid" (Psalm 27:1).

- *Read* the text
- *Think* about what you have just read.
- *Meditate* on the words and message of the text.
- What is God saying to you in this text?
- I hear God saying:

_____
_____
_____
_____
_____
_____
_____
_____
_____
_____

Pray the text back to God.

Engage in a three-to-five-minute meditation if you are at home. However, in a church or retreat setting, two to three minutes will work. Meditate and listen to God speaking to you.

How would your response to fear be different after reading this text?

_____
_____
_____
_____
_____
_____
_____
_____

108  When God Turns Our Mourning into Joy

_____
_____
_____

Sing a song that matches the message that you have just received from God. Or you may listen to pre-recorded music, a CD, or DVD of the song that matches what God is saying to you.

**Hymn**: #519 (*Seventh-day Adventist Hymnal*)—*Give to the Winds Your Fears*

**Text**: "In all thy ways acknowledge Him, and He shall direct your paths" (Proverbs 3:6).

- *Read* the text
- *Think* about what you have just read.
- *Meditate* on the words and message of the text.
- What is God saying to you in this text?
- I hear God saying:

_____
_____
_____
_____
_____
_____
_____
_____
_____
_____
_____
_____

Pray the text back to God.

Engage in a three-to-five-minute meditation if you are at home. However, in a church or retreat setting, two to three minutes will work. Meditate and listen to God speaking to you.

How would your life be different if you allowed God to direct your paths? Is there any aspect of your life that you need to submit to God?

_____
_____
_____
_____
_____
_____
_____
_____
_____
_____
_____
_____

Sing a song that matches the message that you have just received from God. Or you may listen to pre-recorded music, a CD, or DVD of the song that matches what God is saying to you.

**Hymn**: #510 (*Seventh-day Adventist Hymnal*)—*If You But Trust in God to Guide You*

**Text**: "The Lord thy God in the midst of thee is mighty; he will save, he will rejoice over thee with joy; he will rest in his love, he will joy over thee with singing" (Zephaniah 3:17).

- *Read* the text
- *Think* about what you have just read.
- *Meditate* on the words and message of the text.
- What is God saying to you in this text?
- I hear God saying:

_____
_____
_____
_____
_____

# 110  When God Turns Our Mourning into Joy

_____
_____
_____
_____
_____
_____

Pray the text back to God.

Engage in a three-to-five-minute meditation if you are at home. However, in a church or retreat setting, two to three minutes will work. Meditate and listen to God speaking to you.

What images came to mind while reading this text and listening to God to speak to you?

Draw the images that came to your mind. Or if you prefer to write them, do so now.

_____
_____
_____
_____
_____
_____
_____
_____
_____
_____
_____

Sing a song that matches the message that you have just received from God. Or you may listen to pre-recorded music, a CD, or DVD of the song that matches what God is saying to you.

Hymn: #535 (*Seventh-day Adventist Hymnal*)—I Am Ttrusting Thee, Lord Jesus

Text: "So Jesus said to them, 'Because of your unbelief; for assuredly, I say to you, if you have faith as a mustard seed, you will say to this mountain,

"Move from here to there,' and it will move; and nothing will be impossible for you'" (Matthew 17:20, NKJV).

- *Read* the text
- *Think* about what you have just read.
- *Meditate* on the words and message of the text.
- What is God saying to you in this text?
- I hear God saying:

_____
_____
_____
_____
_____
_____
_____
_____
_____
_____

Pray the text back to God.

Engage in a three-to-five-minute meditation if you are at home. However, in a church or retreat setting, two to three minutes will work. Meditate and listen to God speaking to you.

After listening to God speak to you, draw a picture to illustrate your experience with God. Or write a song, poem, or story to illustrate your experience.

_____
_____
_____
_____
_____
_____
_____

## When God Turns Our Mourning into Joy

_____
_____
_____
_____

Sing a song that matches the message that you have just received from God. Or you may listen to pre-recorded music, a CD, or DVD of the song that matches what God is saying to you.

Hymn: #510 (*Seventh-day Adventist Hymnal*)—*If You But Trust in God to Guide You*

**Text**: "Finally, my brethren, be strong in the Lord and the power of His might. Put on the whole armor of God that you may be able to stand against the wiles of the devil" (Ephesian 6:10–11, NKJV).

- *Read* the text
- *Think* about what you have just read.
- *Meditate* on the words and message of the text.
- What is God saying to you in this text?
- I hear God saying:

_____
_____
_____
_____
_____
_____
_____
_____
_____
_____

Pray the text back to God.

## Chapter 18 God's Faithfulness

Engage in a three-to-five-minute meditation if you are at home. However, in a church or retreat setting, two to three minutes will work. Meditate and listen to God speaking to you.

Draw a picture to illustrate the image that just came to mind after meditating and listening to God.

Sing a song that matches the message that you have just received from God. Or you may listen to pre-recorded music, a CD, or DVD of the song that matches what God is saying to you.

Hymn: #529 (*Seventh-day Adventist Hymnal*)—*Under His Wings*

**Text**: "I can do all things through Christ who strengthens me" (Philippians 4:13, NKJV).

- *Read* the text
- *Think* about what you have just read.
- *Meditate* on the words and message of the text.
- What is God saying to you in this text?
- I hear God saying:

_____
_____
_____
_____
_____
_____
_____
_____
_____
_____
_____
_____

Pray the text back to God.

Engage in a three-to-five-minute meditation if you are at home. However, in a church or retreat setting, two to three minutes meditation will work. Listen to God speaking to you.

# 114   When God Turns Our Mourning into Joy

What imagery came to your mind as you read, prayed, and meditated on the text?

Draw the image that is in your mind.

Sing a song that matches the message that you have just received from God. Alternatively, you may listen to pre-recorded music, a CD, or DVD of the song that matches what God is saying to you.

Hymn: #309 (*Seventh-day Adventist Hymnal*)—*I Surrender All*

**Text**: "But Jesus beheld them, and said unto them, With men this is impossible; but with God all things are possible" (Matthew 19:26).

- *Read* the text
- *Think* about what you have just read.
- *Meditate* on the words and message of the text.
- What is God saying to you in this text?
- I hear God saying:

_____
_____
_____
_____
_____
_____
_____
_____
_____
_____
_____
_____

Pray the text back to God.

Engage in a three-to-five-minute meditation if you are at home. However, in a church or retreat setting, two to three minutes will work. Meditate and listen to God speaking to you.

# Chapter 18 God's Faithfulness 115

Write one word that comes to mind after reading the text, praying, meditating, and listening to God. Why did you choose that word?

_____
_____
_____
_____
_____
_____
_____
_____
_____
_____
_____
_____
_____

Sing a song that matches the message that you have just received from God. Alternatively, you may listen to pre-recorded music, a CD, or DVD of the song that matches what God is saying to you.

Hymn: #524 (*Seventh-day Adventist Hymnal*)—*'Tis So Sweet to Trust in Jesus*

**Text**: "Have not I commanded you? Be strong and of good courage; do not be afraid,

- *Read* the text
- *Think* about what you have just read.
- *Meditate* on the words and message of the text.
- What is God saying to you in this text?
- I hear God saying:

_____
_____
_____
_____
_____
_____
_____

_____

_____

_____

_____

_____

Pray the text back to God.

Engage in a three-to-five-minute meditation if you are at home. However, in a church or retreat setting, two to three minutes meditation will work. Listen to God speaking to you.

Identify the five most powerful words in the verse.

1.

2.

3.

4.

5.

Sing a song that matches the message that you have just received from God. Alternatively, you may listen to pre-recorded music, a CD, or DVD of the song that matches what God is saying to you.

Hymn: #100 (*Seventh-day Adventist Hymnal*)—*Great Is Thy Faithfulness*

*Chapter 19*
# *Confidence in God Against all Odds*

**Text**: "Then Esther bade them return Mordecai this answer, 'Go, gather together all the Jews that are present in Shushan, and fast ye for me, and neither eat nor drink three days, night or day: I also and my maidens will fast likewise; and so will I go in unto the king, which is not according to the law: and if I perish, I perish'" (Esther 4:15–16)!

- *Read* the text
- *Think* about what you have just read.
- *Meditate* on the words and message of the text.
- What is God saying to you in this text?
- I hear God saying:

_____
_____
_____
_____
_____

Pray the text back to God.

Engage in a three-to-five-minute meditation if you are at home. However, in a church or retreat setting, two to three minutes will work. Meditate and listen to God speaking to you.

How would your life be different if you heeded the counsels in the text?

Sing a song that matches the message that you have just received from God. Alternatively, you may listen to pre-recorded music, a CD, or DVD of the song that matches what God is saying to you.

Hymn: *#279 (Seventh-day Adventist Hymnal)—Only Trust Him*

*Chapter 20*
# *Abiding in His Presence*

**Text**: "And coming at that instant she gave thanks to the Lord, and spoke of Him to all those who looked for redemption in Jerusalem" (Luke 2:38, NKJV).

- *Read* the text
- *Think* about what you have just read.
- *Meditate* on the words and message of the text.
- What is God saying to you in this text?
- I hear God saying:

_____
_____
_____
_____
_____
_____
_____
_____

Pray the text back to God.

Engage in a three-to-five-minute meditation if you are at home. However, in a church or retreat setting, two to three minutes will work. Meditate and listen to God speaking to you.

What benefits are derived from faithfulness in Jesus?

Sing a song that matches the message that you have just received from God. Or you may listen to pre-recorded music, a CD, or DVD of the song that matches what God is saying to you.

Hymn: #602 (*Seventh-day Adventist Hymnal*)—*O Brother, Be Faithful*

*Chapter 21*

# The Secret to Spiritual Wellness

**Text**: "He shall cover you with His feathers, and under His wings you shall take refuge; His truth shall be your shield and buckler" (Psalm 91:4, NKJV).

- *Read* the text

- *Think* about what you have just read.

- *Meditate* on the words and message of the text.

- What is God saying to you in this text?

- I hear God saying:

_____
_____
_____
_____
_____
_____
_____

_____
_____
_____
_____
_____

Sing the song that the Holy Spirit impresses upon your heart during the meditation.

Pray the text back to God.

How will your life be different when you live everyday under the protecting wings of Jesus?

_____
_____
_____
_____
_____
_____
_____
_____
_____
_____

**Text**: " No weapon that is formed against thee shall prosper; and every tongue that shall rise against thee in judgment thou shalt condemn. This is the heritage of the servants of the Lord, and their righteousness is of me, saith the Lord" (Isaiah 54:17).

- *Read* the text twice, focusing on the key words.
- *Think* about what you have just read.
- *Meditate* on the words and message of the text.
- What is God saying to you in this text?
- I hear God saying:

## Chapter 21  The Secret to Spiritual Wellness

Sing a song that reflects what God is saying to you.

**Text**: "Hear my cry, O God; attend unto my prayer. From the end of the earth will I cry unto thee, when my heart is overwhelmed; lead me to the rock that is higher than I" (Psalms 61:1–2).

Compare and contrast the messages in Isaiah 54:17 with those in Psalms 61:1–2.

Sing a song or listen to recorded music that reflects the messages in the texts. What is God saying to you in these verses?

## When God Turns Our Mourning into Joy

_____
_____
_____
_____
_____
_____
_____
_____
_____

Pray the texts back to God.

Draw a picture that illustrates what God is saying to you after reading, singing, and listening to God.

**Text**: "Bless the Lord, O my soul: and all that is within me, bless His holy name. Bless the Lord, O my soul, and forget not all His benefits: Who forgiveth all thine iniquities; who healeth all thy diseases; who redeemed thy life from destruction; who crowneth thee with lovingkindness and tender mercies; who satisfieth thy mouth with good things; so that thy youth is renewed like the eagle's" (Psalm 103:1–5).

- *Read* the text.
- *Read* the text again, identifying the key words.
- *Think* about what you have just read.
- *Meditate* on the words and message of the text.
- What is God saying to you in this text?
- I hear God saying:

_____
_____
_____
_____
_____
_____
_____

Sing a song that matches the message that God just gave to you.

Read the text again, meditating on the message that God is sharing with you.

Sing a song that reflects what you have heard again from the Lord.

Pray the text back to God.

How would your life be different in the coming week as a result of this text, message from the Lord, and songs that you have just sung?

**Text**: "This I say then, walk in the Spirit, and ye shall not fulfil the lust of the flesh. For the flesh lusteth against the Spirit, and the Spirit against the flesh; and these are contrary the one to the other: so that ye cannot do the things that ye would. However, if ye be led of the Spirit, ye are not under the law" (Galatians 5:16–17).

- *Read* the text.
- *Read* the text again, identifying the key words.
- *Think* about what you have just read.
- *Meditate* on the words and message of the text.
- What is God saying to you in this text?

- I hear God saying:

_____
_____
_____
_____
_____
_____
_____
_____
_____
_____
_____
_____

Sing a song to reflect what you need God to do for you right now (fill me now).

Illustrate the message in the text using three images—(1) person struggling with sin, (2) old man, (3) Holy Spirit.

You want to serve God but the struggles of life keep you from enjoying life in Jesus.

God is not giving up on you; He continues to struggle with you to redeem you unto Himself. Feeling the conviction of the Holy Spirit, you surrender to God, giving the flesh over to His control and bury the old man.

Now you read the Bible daily, walk in the Spirit, go to church, love and respect your spouse, etc. Sin no longer has control over you; the flesh is buried under the power of the Holy Spirit.

Read the texts again. Sing the songs that reflect your meditation and what God is doing for you right now.

What is God saying to you in this text?

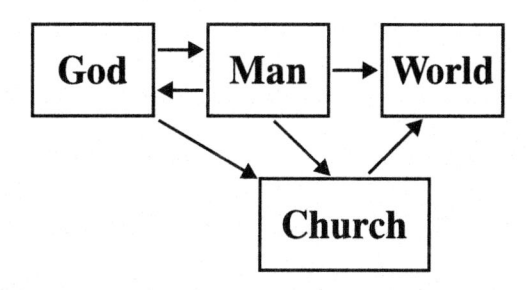

I hear God saying:

_____
_____
_____
_____
_____
_____
_____
_____
_____
_____
_____
_____

Pray the text back to God.

```
┌─────┐ → ┌─────┐ → ┌───────┐
│ God │ ← │ Man │   │ World │
└─────┘   └─────┘   └───────┘
      ↘     ↓     ↗
        ┌────────┐
        │ Church │
        └────────┘
```

Engage in a three-to-five-minute meditation if you are at home. However, in a church or retreat setting, engage in two to three minutes meditation and listen to God speaking to you.

Sing a song that matches the message that you have just received from God. Alternatively, you may listen to pre-recorded music, a CD, or DVD of the song that matches what God is saying to you.

**Text**: "O God you are my God; early will I seek you; my soul thirsts for you; my flesh longs for you in a dry and thirsty land where there is no water. So I have looked for you in the sanctuary, to see your power and your glory" (Psalm 63:1–2).

- *Read* the text
- *Think* about what you have just read.
- *Meditate* on the words and message of the text.
- What is God saying to you in this text?
- I hear God saying:

_____
_____
_____
_____
_____
_____
_____
_____
_____
_____

Pray the text back to God.

Draw a picture to illustrate what God is saying to you in the text.

Engage in a three-to-five-minute meditation if you are at home. However, in a church or retreat setting, two to three minutes will work. Meditate and listen to God speaking to you.

When we behold God, we discover who God is. We enter into the scantuary to experience His power and love. Our soul longs for God.

Read the text again. How many will want to see God in His scantuary?

Read the text once more, emphasizing the key words—early, seek, thirsteth, etc.

Sing a song that matches the message that you have just received from God. Or you may listen to pre-recorded music, a CD, or DVD of the song that matches what God is saying to you.

**Text**: Psalm 51:1–13

Read the verses, pause at powerful junctures, and sing songs to reflect your experience with God right now:

1. Verses 1 to 2: "Have mercy upon me, O God, according to thy lovingkindness: according unto the multitude of thy tender mercies blot out my transgressions. Wash me throughly from mine iniquity, and cleanse me from my sin."

Sing

2. Verses 3 to 6: "For I acknowledge my transgressions: and my sin is ever before me. Against thee, thee only, have I sinned, and done this evil in thy sight: that thou mightest be justified when thou speakest, and be clear when thou judgest. Behold, I was shapen in iniquity; and in sin did my mother conceive me. Behold, thou desirest truth in the inward parts: and in the hidden part thou shalt make me to know wisdom."

Sing

3. Verses 7 to 9: "Purge me with hyssop, and I shall be clean: wash me, and I shall be whiter than snow. Make me to hear joy and gladness; that the bones which thou hast broken may rejoice. Hide thy face from my sins, and blot out all mine iniquities."

Sing

4. Verses 10 to 13: "Create in me a clean heart, O God; and renew a right spirit within me. Cast me not away from thy presence; and take not thy holy spirit from me. Restore unto me the joy of thy salvation; and uphold me with thy free spirit. Then will I teach transgressors thy ways; and sinners shall be converted unto thee."

Sing

Engage in prayer sessions using the PART prayer

P—*praise* God for who He is.
   Sing *Revive Us Again with Power From on High*
A—*adore* God for who He is.
   Sing *Whiter Than Snow* (#318—*Seventh-day Adventist Hymnal*)
R—*request* in silence your desires of God.
   Sing *Whiter Than Snow* (#318—*Seventh-day Adventist Hymnal*)
T—*thank* God for what He has done for you.
   Sing *Lord, I Want to Be a Christian* (#319— *Seventh-day Adventist Hymnal*)
Meditate on your experience with God.

*Chapter 22*
# *The Joy of Surrender*

**Text**: "And Hezekiah received the letter from the hand of the messengers and read it, and Hezekiah went up to the house of the Lord and spread it before the Lord" (Isaiah 37:14).

- *Read* the text
- *Think* about what you have just read.
- *Meditate* on the words and message of the text.
- What is God saying to you in this text?
- I hear God saying:

_____
_____
_____
_____
_____
_____
_____

## 132  When God Turns Our Mourning into Joy

_____
_____
_____
_____
_____

Pray the text back to God.

Engage in a three-to-five-minute meditation if you are at home. However, in a church or retreat setting, two to three minutes will work. Meditate and listen to God speaking to you.

Draw a picture to illustrate what happens when you release your problem to God.

Sing a song that matches the message that you have just received from God. Alternatively, you may listen to pre-recorded music, a CD, or DVD of the song that matches what God is saying to you.

**Text**: "Have you not known? Have you not heard? The everlasting God, the Lord, the Creator of the ends of the earth, neither faints nor is weary. His understanding is unsearchable. He gives power to the weak, and to those who have no might, He increases strength" (Isaiah 40:28–29, NKJV).

- *Read* the text
- *Think* about what you have just read.
- *Meditate* on the words and message of the text.
- What is God saying to you in this text?
- I hear God saying:

_____
_____
_____
_____
_____
_____
_____
_____
_____

# Chapter 22 The Joy of Surrender 133

_____
_____

Pray the text back to God.

Engage in a three-to-five-minute meditation if you are at home. However, in a church or retreat setting, two to three minutes will work. Meditate and listen to God speaking to you.

Sing a song that matches the message that you have just received from God. Alternatively, you may listen to pre-recorded music, a CD, or DVD of the song that matches what God is saying to you.

How would your life be different after God increased your strength and renewed your life?

Draw a picture here to illustrate your life after experiencing renewal.

**Text**: "But they that wait upon the Lord shall renew their strength; they shall mount up with wings as eagles; they shall run, and not be weary; and they shall walk, and not faint" (Isaiah 40: 31).

- *Read* the text
- *Think* about what you have just read.
- *Meditate* on the words and message of the text.
- What is God saying to you in this text?
- I hear God saying:

_____
_____
_____
_____
_____
_____
_____
_____
_____
_____
_____
_____

## 134   When God Turns Our Mourning into Joy

Pray the text back to God.

Sing a song that matches the message that you have just received from God. Or you may listen to pre-recorded music, a CD, or DVD of the song that matches what God is saying to you.

Write a one verse poem, acrostic, rhyme, or song to express how you feel when waiting on God.

What benefits have you gained from waiting on God?

**Text**: "Those things which ye have both learned, and received, and heard, and seen in me, do: and the God of peace shall be with you" (Philippians 4:9).

- *Read* the text
- *Think* about what you have just read.
- *Meditate* on the words and message of the text.
- What is God saying to you in this text?
- I hear God saying:

_____
_____
_____
_____
_____
_____
_____
_____
_____
_____
_____
_____

Pray the text back to God.

Sing a song that matches the message that you have just received from God. Or you may listen to pre-recorded music, a CD, or DVD of the song that matches what God is saying to you.

# Chapter 22 The Joy of Surrender

Draw a picture to express the results of doing what you've learned, received, and heard from God.

**Text**: "Who is a wise man and endued with knowledge among you? Let him shew out of a good conversation his works with meekness of wisdom" (James 3:13).

- *Read* the text
- *Think* about what you have just read.
- *Meditate* on the words and message of the text.
- What is God saying to you in this text?
- I hear God saying:

_____
_____
_____
_____
_____
_____
_____
_____
_____
_____
_____
_____

Ask God to endow you with wisdom and knowledge.

Sing a song that matches the message that you have just received from God. Or you may listen to pre-recorded music, CD, or DVD of the song that matches what God is saying to you.

Write three ways in which you will be able to minister to others after receiving wisdom and knowledge from God.

1.

2.

3.

**Text**: "Teach me to do thy will; for thou art my God: thy spirit is good; lead me into the land of uprightness" (Psalm 143:10).

- *Read* the text
- *Think* about what you have just read.
- *Meditate* on the words and message of the text.
- What is God saying to you in this text?
- I hear God saying:

_____
_____
_____
_____
_____
_____
_____
_____
_____
_____
_____

Pray the text back to God.

Sing a song that matches the message that you have just received from God. Or you may listen to pre-recorded music that matches what God is saying to you.

Draw a picture to illustrate what your life will be like after God teaches you His will and you experience His leading.

What are you going to do now?

**Text**: "Being confident of this very thing, that he which hath begun a good work in you will perform it until the day of Jesus Christ" (Philippians 1:6).

- *Read* the text
- *Think* about what you have just read.
- *Meditate* on the words and message of the text.

# Chapter 22  The Joy of Surrender

- What is God saying to you in this text?
- I hear God saying:

_____
_____
_____
_____
_____
_____
_____
_____
_____
_____
_____
_____
_____

Pray the text back to God.

Sing a song that matches the message that you have just received from God. Or you may listen to pre-recorded music that matches what God is saying to you.

How is your confidence in God's ability to continue doing a good thing in your life?

On a scale of 1 to 10, rate your confidence in God's ability to continue the good work that He started in you: ____

How will your life be different now after rating your confidence in God's ability to continue performing good things on your behalf?

Write four ways that your life will change as a result of your confidence in God.

1.

2.

3.

4.

**Text**: "In whom we have redemption through his blood, the forgiveness of sins, according to the riches of his grace" (Ephesians 1:7).

- *Read* the text
- *Think* about what you have just read.
- *Meditate* on the words and message of the text.
- What is God saying to you in this text?
- I hear God saying:

_____
_____
_____
_____
_____
_____
_____
_____
_____
_____
_____
_____

Pray the text back to God.

Sing a song that matches the message that you have just received from God. Or you may listen to pre-recorded music.

*Chapter 23*
# *Finding Pleasure in Trusting*

**Text**: "For we have no power against this great multitude that is coming against us; nor do we know what to do, but our eyes are upon you" (2 Chronicles 20:12, NKJV).

- *Read* the text

- *Think* about what you have just read.

- *Meditate* on the words and message of the text.

- What is God saying to you in this text?

- I hear God saying:

_____
_____
_____
_____
_____
_____
_____

_____
_____
_____
_____
_____

Pray the text back to God.

Engage in a three-to-five-minute meditation if you are at home. However, in a church or retreat setting, two to three minutes will work. Meditate and listen to God speaking to you.

Sing a song that matches the message that you have just received from God. Or you may listen to pre-recorded music, a CD, or DVD of the song that matches what God is saying to you.

**Text**: "Remember ye not the former things, neither consider the things of old. Behold, I will do a new thing; now it shall spring forth; shall ye not know it? I will even make a way in the wilderness, and rivers in the desert" (Isaiah 43:18–19).

- *Read* the text
- *Think* about what you have just read.
- *Meditate* on the words and message of the text.
- What is God saying to you in this text?
- I hear God saying:

_____
_____
_____
_____
_____
_____
_____
_____
_____
_____

# Chapter 23 Finding Pleasure in Trusting

Pray the text back to God.

Engage in a three-to-five-minute meditation if you are at home. However, in a church or retreat setting, two to three minutes will work. Meditate and listen to God speaking to you.

Sing a song that matches the message that you have just received from God. Or you may listen to pre-recorded music, a CD, or DVD of the song that matches what God is saying to you.

**Text**: "By faith the harlot Rahab perished not with them that believed not, when she had received the spies with peace" (Hebrews 11:31).

- *Read* the text
- *Think* about what you have just read.
- *Meditate* on the words and message of the text.
- What is God saying to you in this text?
- I hear God saying:

_____
_____
_____
_____
_____
_____
_____
_____
_____
_____
_____
_____
_____

Pray the text back to God.

Engage in a three-to-five-minute meditation if you are at home. However, in a church or retreat setting, two to three minutes will work. Meditate and listen to God speaking to you.

Sing a song that matches the message that you have just received from God. Or you may listen to pre-recorded music, a CD, or DVD of the song that matches what God is saying to you.

**Text**: "So when they had rowed about five and twenty or thirty furlongs, they see Jesus walking on the sea, and drawing nigh unto the ship: and they were afraid. But he saith unto them, it is I; be not afraid" (John 6:19–20).

- *Read* the text
- *Think* about what you have just read.
- *Meditate* on the words and message of the text.
- What is God saying to you in this text?
- I hear God saying:

_____
_____
_____
_____
_____
_____
_____
_____
_____
_____
_____

Pray the text back to God.

Engage in a three-to-five-minute meditation if you are at home. However, in a church or retreat setting, two to three minutes will work. Meditate and listen to God speaking to you.

What experiences have you had that resonate with the messages in the text?

_____
_____
_____
_____

# Chapter 23 Finding Pleasure in Trusting 143

_____
_____
_____
_____
_____
_____
_____
_____

Sing a song that matches the message that you have just received from God. Or you may listen to pre-recorded music, a CD, or DVD of the song that matches what God is saying to you.

**Text**: "The Lord hath appeared of old unto me, saying, Yea, I have loved thee with an everlasting love: therefore, with lovingkindness have I drawn thee"( Jeremiah 31:3).

Read the text.

What does it look and feel like when God enters your presence?

_____
_____
_____
_____
_____
_____
_____
_____
_____
_____
_____
_____

How do you feel when you hear God saying to you, "I have loved thee with an everlasting love; therefore, with lovingkindness have I drawn thee?"

_____
_____
_____
_____
_____

144  When God Turns Our Mourning into Joy

_____
_____
_____
_____
_____
_____
_____

What changes would occur in your life as a result of being in God's presence and hearing Him express everlasting love to you?

_____
_____
_____
_____
_____
_____
_____
_____
_____
_____

Pray the text back to God. Thank Him for the privilege of entering His presence; thank Him also for His love.

Sing a song that matches the message that you have just received from God. Or you may listen to pre-recorded music, a CD, or DVD of the song that matches what God is saying to you.

**Text**: "Cast thy burden upon the Lord, and He shall sustain thee; He shall never suffer the righteous to be moved" (Psalm 55:22).

Read the text.

Tell God about everything that is weighing you down right now. What are the burdens that you have been carrying?

Write your burdens on toilet tissue paper. Spread the tissue paper before God and lift the tissue paper up to Him. Ask Him to take the burdens away from you and cast them in the deepest parts of the earth.

Thank God for taking your burdens. Crush the toilet tissue paper and flush it down the toilet. Never think of them again. God has taken them away from you.

Sing songs of thanksgiving—*Amazing Grace* (#108— *Seventh-day Adventist* Hymnal) and *Victory in Jesus*.

Whenever the devil tries to bring the burdens back to your consciousness, sing these songs of thanksgiving.

How would your life be different now as a result of God taking your burdens and placing them in the inner most parts of the earth?

_____
_____
_____
_____
_____
_____
_____
_____
_____
_____
_____
_____
_____
_____
_____
_____
_____
_____
_____
_____
_____
_____
_____

Sing a song that matches how you are feeling right now. Alternately, you may listen to pre-recorded music, a CD, or DVD of the song that matches what God is saying to you.

## 146 When God Turns Our Mourning into Joy

**Text**: "But ye are a chosen generation, a royal priesthood, an holy nation, a peculiar people; that ye should shew forth the praises of Him who hath called you out of darkness into His marvelous light" (1 Peter 2:9).

Read the text.

Write the keywords in the text.

_____
_____
_____
_____
_____
_____
_____
_____
_____
_____
_____

Think about each keyword that you have written.

Meditate on these words and message of the text.

How is your life going to be different as a result of accepting what God has just called you to?

_____
_____
_____
_____
_____
_____
_____
_____
_____
_____
_____

Pray the text back to God.

Sing a song that matches the message that you have just received from God. Or you may listen to pre-recorded music, a CD, or DVD of the song that matches what God is saying to you.

*Chapter 24*

# *Allowing Him to Forgive Us*

**Text**: "Then I set my face toward the Lord God to make a request by prayer and supplications, with fasting, sackcloth, and ashes. And I prayed to the Lord my God, and made confession, and said, 'O Lord, great and awesome God, who keeps His covenant and mercy with those who love Him, and with those who keep His commandments, we have sinned and committed iniquity, we have done wickedly and rebelled, even by departing from your precepts and your judgments" (Daniel 9:3–5, NKJV).

- *Read* the text

- *Think* about what you have just read.

- *Meditate* on the words and message of the text.

- What is God saying to you in this text?

- I hear God saying:

_____

_____

_____

## Chapter 24  Allowing Him to Forgive Us

_____
_____
_____
_____
_____
_____
_____
_____
_____

Pray the text back to God.

Engage in a three-to-five-minute meditation if you are at home. However, in a church or retreat setting, two to three minutes meditation will work. Listen to God speaking to you. Open your heart to Him and imagine Him sitting next to you.

How do you plan to show forth His love and praises?

_____
_____
_____
_____
_____
_____
_____
_____
_____
_____
_____
_____

Sing a song that matches the message that you have just received from God. Alternatively, you may listen to pre-recorded music, a CD, or DVD of the song that matches what God is saying to you.

**Text**: "In the year that king Uzziah died, I saw the Lord sitting on a throne, high and lifted up, and the train of His robe filled the temple, above it stood seraphim; each one had six wings; with two He covered His face, with two he covered his feet, and with two he flew. And one cried to another and said: 'Holy, holy, holy is the Lord of hosts; the whole earth is full of His

## 150   When God Turns Our Mourning into Joy

glory!' And the posts of the doorwere shaken by the voice of him who cried out, and the house was filled with smoke. So I said: 'Woe is me, for I am undone! Because I am a man of unclean lips; for my eyes have seen the king, the Lord of hosts.' Then one of the seraphim flew to me, having in his hand a live coal which he had taken with the tongs from the altar. And he touched my mouth with it, and said: 'Behold, this has touched your lips; your iniquity is taken away, and your sin purged" (Isaiah 6:1–8).

- *Read* the text
- *Think* about what you have just read.
- *Meditate* on the words and message of the text.
- What is God saying to you in this text?
- I hear God saying:

_____
_____
_____
_____
_____
_____
_____
_____
_____
_____
_____

What are the four principles of transformation in the text?

1. Principle 1 (vs 1–4):
2. Principle 2 (v 5):
3. Principle 3 (v 6):
4. Principle 4 (vs 7–9):

When we behold God, our minds turn upward to God to see Jesus standing in the midst of the candlesticks.

## Chapter 24 Allowing Him to Forgive Us 151

When we see Jesus, our hearts melt and respond to God as we express our experience of forgiveness.

Sing a song that reflects what God has done for you.

Pray a prayer to demonstrate God's transformation in your heart.

Testify of God's goodness to you right now.

Write your testimony to God here.

_____
_____
_____
_____
_____
_____
_____
_____
_____
_____
_____
_____

Sing a song that reflects God's goodness to you.

**Text**: "Let all bitterness, wrath, anger, clamor, and evil speaking be put away from you, with all malice. And be kind to one another, tenderhearted, forgiving one another, even as God in Christ forgave you" (Ephesians 4:31–32).

- *Read* the text
- *Think* about what you have just read.
- *Meditate* on the words and message of the text.
- What is God saying to you in this text?
- I hear God saying:

_____
_____
_____

## When God Turns Our Mourning into Joy

_____
_____
_____
_____
_____
_____
_____
_____
_____

Illustrate the message in the text:

Person 1 represents a member, Person 2 represents God, and Person 3 represents a friend in the community.

Member is guilty of sin, kneels, lifts his hands to God and asks for forgiveness. God hears and forgives Him, offers His gift of grace.

Forgiveness is for the wrongdoer and the recipient. God forgave me, and I forgave you.

Forgiveness brings spiritual, emotional, and physical healing.

Pray a prayer for forgiveness now.

Sing a song that expresses God's transformation and forgiveness in your life.

**Text**: "To console those who mourn in Zion, to give them beauty for ashes, the oil of joy for mourning, the garment of praise for the spirit of heaviness; that they may be called trees of righteousness, the planting of the Lord, that He may be glorified" (Isaiah 61:3, NKJV).

- *Read* the text.
- *Read* the text again, identifying the key words.
- *Think* about what you have just read.
- *Meditate* on the words and message of the text.
- What is God saying to you in this text?
- I hear God saying:

# Chapter 24 Allowing Him to Forgive Us 153

_____
_____
_____
_____
_____
_____
_____
_____
_____
_____
_____
_____
_____

Explain the text to someone next to you or write in your reflective journal what you understand in the text. Or write the message that you received from God.

Pray the text back to God.

God places before us two choices:

| Satan gaves us: | Jesus takes the ashes and gives us: |
|---|---|
| Burnt ashes | Beauty |
| Bitterness | Productivity |
| Mourning | Joy |
| Spirit of heaviness | Consolation, oil of joy |
|  | Spirit of praise |
|  | Righteousness |
|  | Growth |
|  | Success |

Sing songs that express God's forgiveness towards you.

Hymn: #485 (*Seventh-day Adventist Hymnal*)—*I Must Tell Jesus*

**Text**: Moreover if your brother sins against you. Go and tell him his fault between you and him alone. If he hears you, you have gained your brother. But if he will not hear, take with you one or two more, that by the mouth of two or three witnesses every word may be established; and if he refuses to hear them, tell it to the church, let him be to you like a heathen and a tax collector...so my heavenly Father also will do to you if each of you, from his heart, does not forgive his brother his trespasses" (Matthew 18:15–35, NKJV).

- *Read* the text
- *Think* about what you have just read.
- *Meditate* on the words and message of the text.
- What is God saying to you in this text?
- I hear God saying:

_____
_____
_____
_____
_____
_____
_____
_____
_____
_____
_____

Hymn: #322 (*Seventh-day Adventist Hymnal*)—*Nothing Between My Soul and My Savior*

Sing a song of your choice

Read the following promises, claiming God's forgiveness:

Psalms 113:17
Isaiah 43:3
Isaiah 41:10
Joshua 22:5
Psalm 27:1
Psalm 34:7

## Chapter 24 Allowing Him to Forgive Us

Engage in the concert of prayer, reading Scriptures of praise, confession, pleading with God, and responding to His grace, forgiveness, and cleansing.

Praise
    Psalm 138:1–5
    Psalm 145:1–8
    Psalm 146:1–3
    Psalm 148:1–4
    Psalm 150:1–6
    Psalm 66:1–8

Confession
    Psalm 139:1–8
    Psalm 121:1–8
    Psalm 51:1–10
    Psalm 32:1–5
    Psalm 15:1–3

Pleading with God
    Psalm 69:1–8
    Psalm 70:1–5
    Psalm 74:1–8
    Psalm 109:1–54

Thanksgiving
    Psalm 105:1–5
    Psalm 107:1–3

Response
    Psalm 37:1–8
    Isaiah 63:3
    Matthew 18:21–35

Sing: *Nothing Between My Soul and My Savior* (see above).

*Chapter 25*

# Experiencing His Restoration

**Text**: "Ah, Lord God! Behold, You have made the heavens and the earth by your great power and outstretched arm. There is nothing too hard for You...'Behold, I am the Lord of all flesh. Is there anything too hard for Me'" (Jeremiah 32:17, 27, NKJV)?

- *Read* the text
- *Think* about what you have just read.
- *Meditate* on the words and message of the text.
- What is God saying to you in this text?
- I hear God saying:

_____
_____
_____
_____
_____
_____

## Chapter 25  Experiencing His Restoration    157

_____
_____
_____
_____
_____

Pray the text back to God.

Engage in a three-to-five-minute meditation if you are at home. However, in a church or retreat setting, two to three minutes will work. Meditate and listen to God speaking to you.

Sing a song that matches the message that you have just received from God. Alternatively, you may listen to pre-recorded music, a CD, or DVD of the song that matches what God is saying to you.

What would you like God to restore unto you?

Tell God what you need Him to restore.

Write them here.

_____
_____
_____
_____
_____
_____
_____
_____
_____
_____
_____

Pray a one-sentence prayer claiming that restoration.

Thank God for the restoration that you have just received.

**Text**:, "Fear ye not, neither be afraid: have not I told thee from that time, and have declared it? Ye are my witnesses. Is there a God beside me? Ye, there is no God; I know not any" (Isaiah 44:8).

- *Read* the text

- *Think* about what you have just read.

- *Meditate* on the words and message of the text.

- What is God saying to you in this text?

- I hear God saying:

_____
_____
_____
_____
_____
_____
_____
_____
_____
_____

Pray the text back to God.

Engage in a three-to-five-minute meditation if you are at home. However, in a church or retreat setting, two to three minutes will work. Meditate and listen to God speaking to you.

Sing a song that matches the message that you have just received from God. Or you may listen to pre-recorded music, a CD, or DVD of the song that matches what God is saying to you.

**Text**: "In thee, O Lord, do I put my trust; let me never be ashamed: deliver me in thy righteousness. Bow down thine ear to me; deliver me speedily: be thou my strong rock, for an house of defense to save me. For thou art my rock and my fortress; therefore for thy name's sake lead me, and guide me. Pull me out of the net that they have laid privily for me: for thou art my strength. Into thine hand I commit my spirit: thou has redeemed me, O Lord God of truth. I have hated them that regard lying vanities: but I trust in the Lord. I will be glad and rejoice in thy mercy: for thou has considered my trouble; thou has known my soul in adversities" (Psalm 31:1–7).

- *Read* the text

## Chapter 25 Experiencing His Restoration

- *Think* about what you have just read.
- *Meditate* on the words and message of the text.
- What is God saying to you in this text?
- I hear God saying:

_____
_____
_____
_____
_____
_____
_____
_____
_____
_____
_____
_____

Pray the text back to God.

Engage in a three-to-five-minute meditation if you are at home. However, in a church or retreat setting, two to three minutes will work. Meditate and listen to God speaking to you.

Sing a song that matches the message that you have just received from God. Or you may listen to pre-recorded music, a CD, or DVD of the song that matches what God is saying to you.

**Text**: "Now unto him that is able to do exceeding abundantly above all that we ask or think, according to the power that worketh in us" (Ephesians 3:20).

- *Read* the text
- *Think* about what you have just read.
- *Meditate* on the words and message of the text.
- What is God saying to you in this text?
- I hear God saying:

Pray the text back to God.

Engage in a three-to-five-minute meditation if you are at home. However, in a church or retreat setting, two to three minutes will work. Meditate and listen to God speaking to you.

Sing a song that matches the message that you have just received from God. Or you may listen to pre-recorded music, a CD, or DVD of the song that matches what God is saying to you.

**Text**: "And I will make an everlasting covenant with them, that I will not turn away from them, to do them good; but I will put my fear in their hearts so that they will not depart from me" (Jeremiah 32:40).

- *Read* the text
- *Think* about what you have just read.
- *Meditate* on the words and message of the text.
- What is God saying to you in this text?
- I hear God saying:

## Chapter 25 Experiencing His Restoration

_____
_____
_____

Pray using this order:

**P**—praise

Sing a song that reflects your praise of God.

**A**—adoration

Sing a song that gives worship to God.

**R**—request

Sing a song that reflects your requests to God.

**T**—thanksgiving

Sing a song that expresses thanksgiving to God.

Sing a song that matches the message that you have just received from God. Alternatively, you may listen to pre-recorded music, a CD, or DVD of the song that matches what God is saying to you.

**Text**: "Yea, I will rejoice over them to do them good, and I will plant them in this land assuredly with my whole heart and with my whole soul" (Jeremiah 32:41).

- *Read* the text
- *Think* about what you have just read.
- *Meditate* on the words and message of the text.
- What is God saying to you in this text?
- I hear God saying:

_____
_____
_____
_____
_____

# 162  When God Turns Our Mourning into Joy

_____
_____
_____
_____
_____

Pray the text back to God.

Engage in a three-to-five-minute meditation if you are at home. However, in a church or retreat setting, two to three minutes will work. Meditate and listen to God speaking to you.

Sings songs that reflect your praise to God for rejoicing over you, to do you good. Alternatively, you may listen to pre-recorded music, a CD, or DVD of the song that matches what God is saying to you.

Engage in testimony for what God has done for you during this prayer experience.

If you are in private devotion, write your testimony here.

# Chapter 25 Experiencing His Restoration 163

---

**Text**: "But as it is written, eye hath not seen, nor ear heard, neither have entered into the heart of man, the things which God hath prepared for them that love him" (1 Corinthians 2:9).

- *Read* the text
- *Think* about what you have just read.
- *Meditate* on the words and message of the text.
- What is God saying to you in this text?
- I hear God saying:

_____
_____
_____
_____
_____
_____
_____
_____
_____
_____

Pray the text back to God.

Sing a song that matches the message that you have just received from God. Or you may listen to pre-recorded music that matches what God is saying to you.

**Text**: "For God hath not given us the spirit of fear; but of power, and of love, and of a sound mind" (2 Timothy 1:7).

- *Read* the text
- *Think* about what you have just read.
- *Meditate* on the words and message of the text.
- What is God saying to you in this text?

164     When God Turns Our Mourning into Joy

- I hear God saying:

_____
_____
_____
_____
_____
_____
_____
_____
_____
_____

How will you manage fear now?

Pray the text back to God.

Sing songs of deliverance and thanksgiving to God. Or you may listen to pre-recorded music, a CD, or DVD of the song that matches what God is saying to you.

**Text**: "Nay, in all these things we are more than conquerors through him that loved us" (Romans 8:37).

- *Read* the text
- *Think* about what you have just read.
- *Meditate* on the words and message of the text.
- What is God saying to you in this text?
- I hear God saying:

_____
_____
_____
_____
_____
_____
_____
_____

Pray the text back to God.

Engage in a three-to-five-minute meditation if you are at home. However, in a church or retreat setting, two to three minutes will work. Listen to God speaking with you.

Sing songs that match the message that you have just received from God. Or you may listen to pre-recorded music, a CD, or DVD of the song that matches what God is saying to you.

**Text**: "So the woman went her way and ate, and her face was no longer sad" (1 Samuel 1:18, NKJV).

- *Read* the text
- *Think* about what you have just read.
- *Meditate* on the words and message of the text.
- What is God saying to you in this text?
- I hear God saying:

_____
_____
_____
_____
_____
_____
_____
_____
_____
_____
_____

Pray the text back to God.

What should your response be after presenting your problems to God?

Engage in a three-to-five-minute meditation if you are at home. However, in a church or retreat setting, two to three minutes will work. Meditate and listen to God speaking to you.

## When God Turns Our Mourning into Joy

Sing songs that match the message that you have just received from God. Or you may listen to pre-recorded music, a CD, or DVD of the song that matches what God is saying to you.

**Text**: "My heart rejoices in the Lord; my horn is exalted in the Lord. I smile at my enemies because I rejoice in your salvation" (1 Samuel 2:1).

- *Read* the text
- *Think* about what you have just read.
- *Meditate* on the words and message of the text.
- What is God saying to you in this text?
- I hear God saying:

_____
_____
_____
_____
_____
_____
_____
_____
_____
_____

Pray the text back to God.

Engage in a three-to-five-minute meditation if you are at home. However, in a church or retreat setting, two to three minutes will work. Meditate and listen to God speaking to you.

Sing songs that match the message that you have just received from God. Or you may listen to pre-recorded music, a CD, or DVD of the song that matches what God is saying to you.

**Text**: "For I know the thoughts that I think toward you, says the Lord, thoughts of peace and not of evil, to give you a future and a hope" (Jeremiah 29:11).

- *Read* the text

## Chapter 25  Experiencing His Restoration

- *Think* about what you have just read.
- *Meditate* on the words and message of the text.
- What is God saying to you in this text?
- I hear God saying:

_____

Pray the text back to God.

Engage in a three-to-five-minute meditation if you are at home. However, in a church or retreat setting, meditate for two to three minutes and listen to God speaking to you.

Sing a song that matches the message that you have just received from God. Or you may listen to pre-recorded music, a CD, or DVD of the song that matches what God is saying to you.

**Text**: "For we walk by faith, not by sight" (2 Corinthians 5:7).

- *Read* the text
- *Think* about what you have just read.
- *Meditate* on the words and message of the text.
- What is God saying to you in this text?
- I hear God saying:

_____

Pray the text back to God.

Engage in a three-to-five-minute meditation if you are at home. However, in a church or retreat setting, two to three minutes will work. Meditate and listen as God speaks to you.

Sing a song that matches the message that you have just received from God. Or you may listen to pre-recorded music, a CD, or DVD of the song that matches what God is saying to you.

**Text**: "Can a woman forget her sucking child, that she should not have compassion on the son of her womb? Yea, they may forget, yet will I not forget you" (Isaiah 49:15).

- *Read* the text
- *Think* about what you have just read.
- *Meditate* on the words and message of the text.
- What is God saying to you in this text?
- I hear God saying:

Pray the text back to God.

Engage in a three-to-five-minute meditation if you are at home. However, in a church or retreat setting, two to three minutes will work. Meditate and listen as God speaks to you.

Sing a song that matches the message that you have just received from God. Or you may listen to pre-recorded music, a CD, or DVD of the song that matches what God is saying to you.

**Text**: "And we know that all things work together for good to them that love God, to them who are the called according to his purpose. For whom he did foreknow, he also did predestinate to be conformed to the image of His son, that he might be the firstborn among many brethren" (Romans 8:28–29).

- *Read* the text
- *Think* about what you have just read.
- *Meditate* on the words and message of the text.
- What is God saying to you in this text?
- I hear God saying:

_____
_____
_____
_____
_____
_____
_____
_____
_____
_____

Pray the text back to God.

Engage in a three-to-five-minute meditation if you are at home. However, in a church or retreat setting, two to three minutes will work. Meditate and listen as God speaks to you.

Sing a song that matches the message that you have just received from God. Or you may listen to pre-recorded music, a CD, or DVD of the song that matches what God is saying to you.

## Conducting A Prayer Retreat in Your Personal Life or the Church

This section of the book will guide you through the process of planning and implementing a one-week prayer revival. It can just be your prayer revival, your family's prayer revival, or a revival in your local church.

*Chapter 26*
# *Approaches For Focusing Your Prayer*

In one sentence, express your prayers to God. Use the part of each acronym to keep your prayer focused.

### ACT

**A**—adoration; lift your voice in adoration to God for who He is (I adore you because you are a mighty healer).

**C**—confession; confess your sins to God (Lord, I confess my wrongdoing to you).

**T**—thanksgiving; thank God for hearing and forgiving you.

### PART

**P**—praise; express praise to God for all that He is to you (Lord I praise you for your transforming power in my life).

**A**—adoration; Lord, I adore you for the loving God that you are.

**R**—request; ask God for what you need right now.

**T**—thanksgiving; thank Him for all that He has done for you.

## **CARTS**

**C**—confession; confess your sins to God silently.

**A**—adoration; pray prayers of adoration for who God is.

**R**—request; submit your requests to God.

**T**—thanksgiving; thank Him for all that He has done for you.

**S**—silence; listen quietly to God, acknowledge His power in your life, and accept His answer to your prayer with confidence. Then, leave the place of prayer with peace in your heart.

## **TARP**

**T**—thanksgiving

**A**—adoration

**R**—rejoicing

**P**—praise

## **STARS**

**S**—spread

**T**—thanksgiving

**A**—acknowledge

**R**—request

**S**—submission

## **PAT**

**P**—praise

**A**—adoration

**T**—thanksgiving

## **FAST**

**F**—fasting

**A**—adoration

**S**—sharing

**T**—thanksgiving

## **FACT**

**F**—fasting

**A**—adoration

**C**—confession

**T**—thanksgiving

*Chapter 27*

# One Week Prayer Retreat

## Sunday: Praise

Turning The Heart Toward God

**Read:** Psalm 37:1–11, then reflect on these phrases. After reflecting on each verse, sing the song which comes to mind from your reflection.

1. "Fret not" (v. 1)
2. "Trust in the Lord" (v. 3)
3. "Delight in the Lord" (v. 4)
4. "Commit your ways" (v. 5)
5. "Rest in the Lord" (v. 7)

Praise God for Who He is:

**Read:** I Chronicles 29:10–12

1. Identify the many attributes of God in these verses.
2. Praise Him in prayer for these attributes.
3. Listen to or sing a song of praise to God.

In Contemplation and Praise before His Throne

**Read:** Revelation 1:12–18

1. Reflect on verse 17.
2. What does praise mean to you?
3. What does praise sound like to you?

My Gifts of Praise

1. What are your reasons for giving praise to God?
2. What are your gifts of praise?
3. How has this praise experience turned your heart toward the Lord?

## Monday: Thanksgiving

*Definition*: the act of giving thanks; grateful acknowledgment of benefits or favors, especially to God. It is an active expression of thanks, especially to God. It can also mean a public celebration in acknowledgment of divine favor or kindness.

What God will do and has done.

**Read**: Jeremiah 33:11–16

1. What will God do in these verses?
2. What or who is the central focus of thanksgiving in these verses?
3. What are you thankful for in verses 15–16?

What God did for us in spite of what we did to Him.

**Read:** Psalm 106:6–9, 9–23, 44–47

1. What evokes thankfulness in your heart?

2. What do these verses tell you about God's love for you?

A Lifestyle of Thanksgiving

**Read:** Psalm 104:4–6

1. Is thankfulness an expression or state of being?
2. What are some ways of giving thanks to the Lord?
3. Where do you enjoy giving thanks to the Lord?

Giving Thanks for The Goodness of God in The Lives of Others

**Read:** Ephesians 1:15–16

1. Reflect–Write–Pray
2. What is God doing in the lives of others for which you wish to thank Him?
3. What is God doing in your life for which you wish to thank him?
4. Sing unto the Lord with all your heart
5. Sing or listen to a song of thanksgiving to the Lord.

## Tuesday: Repentance

*Definition*: A broken and contrite heart in response to God's love

**Read:** 2 Samuel 12:7–9

Question: What are the differences between verses 7–8 and verse 9?

Write: Make list of blessings God has given to you in last five years

Confess: List out to God in silent prayer the sins you committed against Him.

Statement: The Power Of The Goodness Of God In Your Life

**Read:** Romans 2:4

Reflection: How has God treated you differently from how you have treated him?

Draw two contrasting pictures

Question: What disturbs you about these two pictures?

Statement: The Healing Power Of Confession

**Read**: Psalm 51:1–12

Sing or listen to a song that comes to mind after reading those above verses.

Reflection: What causes you to experience godly sorrow?

Write: If you can, describe these feeling.

Statement: Turning To A New Direction

**Read**: 2 Corinthians 5:17

Question: What changes have you decided to make in your life?

Draw: What do changes look like?

Write: Write a short paragraph about your new life in Christ

Read: Read the paragraph to God in the form a prayer.

## Obedience: Wednesday

Jesus was a servant to the Father's will. He "humbled Himself" and became "obedient to the point of death, even the death of the cross" (Phil. 2:8). Jesus provides an example of what a life filled with the Holy Spirit is like. It is a life of willing obedience and humble submission to the Father's will.

Statement: Lives Transformed By The Holy Spirit Produce Obedience.

**Read**: Mathew 26:69–74, Acts 5:28–32

Meditate: Vertical relationship

Question: How was Peter's life in Matthew 26 different from his life in Acts 5?

Reflect: What changes are the Holy Spirit making in your life?

Statement: Obedience inspires commitment to Christ and His mission.

**Read**: Acts 7:54–60

Meditate: Vertical relationship

Question: What was the basis of Steven's obedience and commitment?

Reflection: What would you have done differently from Steven?

Statement: The Holy Spirit Convicts Us Of The Need For A New Life.

**Read**: Acts 9:5–6; 26:28–29

Meditate: Vertical relationship

Question: What are the differences in the above passages?

Reflection: Do you sense the need for a new life in Christ?

Statement: Jesus Lived In Obedience To His Father's Will.

**Read**: Philippians 2:5–8

Meditate: Vertical relationship

Draw: What does obedience look like?

Reflection: How committed are you to doing God's will?

## Thursday: Prayer, Healing, and Restoration

To Identify The Essentials Of Spiritual And Physical Healing

One may logically ask, "Why isn't healing given every time a person seeks God in faith?" The short answer is that every prayer for healing is always answered affirmatively—that is, with a "Yes." The question is not *if* God will heal the sick but *when* He will do it. So, it is not a matter of twisting God's arm but one of timing. Let's explore that concept further. There are three possible moments of timing for divine healing: (1) instantaneous or immediate (as in the case of the paralytic Jesus healed in Matthew 9:1–6); (2) gradual (as in the case of Naaman the leper, in 2 Kings 5); and (3) at the resurrection (as in the case of Paul's "thorn" in the side, or Jacob's hip—see 2 Cor. 12:7; Gen. 32:25). Thus, prayers for healing are always answered affirmatively; it is simply a matter of timing as to when. The decision of timing belongs to God alone as to what will bind us closest to Him and will bring the most glory to His name.

Statement: Prayer And Praise Help Us To Transfer Our Burdens To God

**Read**: James 5:13; Psalm 61:1–2

Question: How can we transfer our burdens to God?

Reflection: What can Jesus give to you in exchange for your burdens?

Statement: The Forgiveness Of Sins Comes Before Physical Healing

**Read**: James 5:14–15

Question: Is your greatest need physical healing or forgiveness of sin?

Reflection: Why have you made this choice?

Pray: Talk to God about this choice.

Note:

How can Jesus' forgiveness make a difference in your health? Healing includes the healing of relationships, which is why we are exhorted to "Confess your faults one to another" (James 5:16), meaning those we have wronged (see Matt. 18:15, 21, 22). That is, if you have wronged or offended others, confess to them. Then the blessing of the Lord will rest upon you because the process of confession involves a dying to self, and only through that death to self can Christ be formed within you.

## Friday: Prayer, Healing and Restoration

Aim: To identify the *essentials* of spiritual and physical healing.

Know: God provides spiritual and physical healing for all people.

Feel: Experience the joy of spiritual and physical healing in Christ.

Do: Trust in Christ for spiritual and physical healing.

Thus, anointing the sick with oil implies that the sick one, even in the midst of affliction, is being set apart so that the Holy Spirit can work

(*Adult Teachers Sabbath School Bible Study Guide*, 4th Quarter 2014, pp. 146–147).

Statement: Prayer And Praise Help Us To Transfer Our Burdens To God

**Read:** James 5:13, Psalm 61:1–2

Meditate: Vertical relationship

Question: How can we transfer our burdens to God?

Share in twos: Horizontal relationship

Application: What should be your response after you tell Jesus all of your troubles?

Statement: The Forgiveness Of Sins Comes Before Physical Healing

**Read**: James 5:14–15

Meditate: Vertical relationship

Question: How is forgiveness related to physical healing?

Share in twos: Horizontal relationship

Application: How can Jesus' forgiveness make a difference in your health? Healing includes the healing of relationships, which is why we are exhorted to "Confess your faults one to another" (James 5:16), meaning those we have wronged (see Matt. 18:15, 21, 22). That is, if you have wronged or offended others, confess to them. Then the blessing of the Lord will rest upon you because the process of confession involves a dying to self, and only through that death to self can Christ be formed within you.

Statement: An Understanding Of Scripture Gives Relevance To Our Prayers

**Read**: Daniel 9:2–3; Deuteronomy 11:13–17

Meditate: Vertical relationship

Question: How did the prophecy of Deuteronomy 11:13–17 inform Elijah's prayer?

Note: Though we do not know how long Elijah prayed before his prayers were answered, his petitions were based on careful study of and reflection upon God's Word in light of his present circumstances. The fervent prayer of a righteous man is always anchored in Scripture.

Statement: Elijah Turned The Hearts Of People Towards God.

**Read** James 5:19–20

Meditate: Vertical relationship

Question: What are the duties of those who are spiritual amongst us?

Share in twos: Horizontal relationship

Application: How can you help a family member to experience forgiveness?

Summary Points:

1. Prayer and praise help us to transfer our burdens to God
2. The forgiveness of sins comes before physical healing
3. An understanding of Scripture gives relevance to our prayers
4. Elijah turned the hearts of people towards God.

## Sabbath: Emotional Healing

What Happens To Our Prayer When We Pray?

For our prayers to be answered, we need God the Father, God the Son, and God the Holy Spirit. Jesus presents our prayers to the Father. Hence the reason why intercessory prayer is necessary. It allows the elders or intercessors to transfer our prayers to God.

How God transforms the lives of people in a prayer conference.

**Read:** Isaiah 6:1–8

Congregation reads the verses, placing emphasis on "Holy! Holy! Holy!"

Process of transformation in our lives

Beholding:

God wanted to send Isaiah on a mission. Isaiah turned his eyes upward to behold the temple. He saw God—His eyes and countenance—among the candlesticks, as well as the twenty-four elders sitting around the throne of God; he looked and beheld the angels worshiping God.

When we behold who Jesus is, we will see who we are. Turn your eyes upon Jesus, and you will grow in glory and grace. When you see who Jesus is, your heart will turn to God. The heart responds to God in three ways: singing, prayer, and testimony. When the mind comes in contact with the mind of God, He transforms the mind. Jesus said that if He is lifted up to God, He will draw all men to Himself (see John 12:32). Turn the minds away from their problems to God. When the mind beholds who God is, the mind turns to God.

Melting:

Woe is me for I am undone.

I am a man of unclean lips, for mine eyes hath seen your glory, I dwell in the midst of a people with unclean lips. Invite the people to read the Word and come in contact with the mind of God. Take them back to the Word; let them see who Jesus is. When the mind is exposed to supernatural power, the heart will respond.

Cleansing:

Paul on the road to Damascus: beheld, melted, cleansed

Peter on the roof top: beheld, melted, cleansed

He had a concept of the process of salvation

Moses in the burning bush: beheld, melted, cleansed

Sending:

When we behold God and experience melting and cleansing, we are motivated to tell others. The woman at the well ran into the village and said, "come see a man."

Read together with emphasis and belief Ephesians 4:31, 32. At the center of these verses is emotional healing. Many persons are sick because of anger, bitterness, and evil speaking. God said let all bitterness, anger, and clamor be put away from you. Why? It will destroy your life. Many years have gone by and you are still bitter about them. Rather, be kind, tender-hearted, and loving, even as Christ has forgiven you.

Illustration: One day, a man went on vacation. Thieves entered into his house and stole his computer, television, many valuables, and $20,000. On his return, he discovered that the house was burgled. He found out who did it. He was angry and bitter towards the thieves. The thieves went enjoying themselves in other things. The thieves and the robbed man all sinned before God. Their consciences are guilty before God. The thieves turn to God and confess their sins before God, kneel before God and ask for forgiveness. God lifts His hands and forgives the thieves. They experience forgiveness and receive the gift of grace. Forgiveness is for the person who has been hurt and wounded. It is for the one wronged, and the one sinned against. Prayer and praise help us to transfer our burdens to God. Because God has forgiven the thief, he in turn forgives those who have sinned against him. The offended turns to God and asks God for forgiveness. God accepts him, and he in turn forgives the one who sinned against him. God has forgiven me, and now I in turn forgive anyone who commits a sin against me. It is lifting a burden from your conscience to be free. It is for the one who has received the hurt. Forgiveness is for healing. God has forgiven me, so I have forgiven you. Forgiveness loosens one from anger, bitterness, and wrath so that he can be healed. God forgives; it is a gift. Many people are sick because of evil speaking, anger, and hurt. God is calling on you to put it away from you.

> *When we behold God and experience melting and cleansing, we are motivated to tell others.*

Call

Who are the people who have hurt you? Said evil against you? Who robbed you?

Today God wants to heal you emotionally and spiritually. God said, "Let all bitterness, wrath, anger, and evil speaking be put away from you." One day, a woman experienced God's forgiveness and decided to forgive the husband who had abused her for many years. Her daughter said no he was too evil. Nevertheless, she called her husband and told him she forgave him. They both wept uncontrollably and received God's forgiveness. Forgiveness is God's way of healing us. Accept God's forgiveness today and be healed.

Sing: Nothing between my soul and the Savior.

Place your hand on your heart. Who are the people who have wronged you? You are the injured one. Go to the person and extend forgiveness to them.

Stand and sing *Amazing Grace* (#108— *Seventh-day Adventist Hymnal*). Because God has healed you, He wants you to extend forgiveness to those who have wronged you.

Sing: *There Is a Fountain* (#336— *Seventh-day Adventist Hymnal*): "There is a fountain filled with blood, drawn from Emmanuel's veins, and sinners plunge beneath that flood lose all their guilty stains." If God has forgiven you, as you sing, raise your hand in recognition to God for His cleansing. Sing emphasizing the word *wash*. Sing the song with emphasis.

Prayer Time:

Bow in prayer. Many persons are here today who have hurt you, injured you, and done evil against you. Go to the person and say, "God has forgiven me, and so I have forgiven you." Eyes are closed as we pray and move to seek forgiveness. Obey God's words and let all evil and bitterness be put away from you. Move as you sing wash all my sins away. There may I though vile as He wash all my sins away.

## Sunday Morning

How God Transforms Human lives

**Read:** John 12:32

Aim: To explain the process of conversion

Do: Contemplate on the life of Jesus through Bible reading

Introduction

The Bible reveals that conversion is a divine act. God encounters the human mind with His glory and love that evokes a genuine response. The sinner responds to a reality that transcends reason. As the sinner beholds the glory of God, he/she is drawn into His divine presence with humility, repentance, confession, and commitment to mission. God begins the conversion process by exposing the sinner to His love, glory, and awesome power. This divine encounter effects changes in the sinner. The sinner experiences a new birth.

> *The Bible reveals that conversion is a divine act.*

The process of conversion includes beholding, melting, cleansing, and sending. This process is illustrated in many passages in the Bible. We see the conversion process in Isaiah 6:1–8, Daniel 3:24–30, Acts 9:1:27, and Revelation 1:12–18. In these passages, conversion begins with God. However, we are participants in the process of conversion. Let us examine this divine and human encounter more carefully in Isaiah 6:1–8.

Beholding: "My eyes have seen."

When we behold who Jesus is, we will see who we are. The glory of God illuminates our consciences to be aware of our sins. Sin becomes offensive to us. The glory of God makes our sin clearer and more repulsive to us. We detest it. Indeed! We see a difference between our old life and what we can become by gazing upon Him. We desire a new life. We confess our sins in His divine presence.

Melting: "Woe is me for I am undone."

God exposes us to His glory to make sin offensive to us. We see the differences between our sins and His glory. God's glory is illuminating, awesome, and spectacular. Our sin, in contrast to His glory, is gruesome, dark, and wearisome. As His glory magnifies our sins, we sense the conviction to turn from and abandon our sins to be accepted into His presence. This is a process of repentance. It is a godly sorrow for sin. The heart is broken and contrite. This state of mind leads us to confess "woe is me, for I am undone."

It is God's love and glory which inspire our confession. Confession is telling God about all the sins we committed and doing so with sorrow. The beloved apostle John says, " If we confess our sins, he is faithful and just to forgive us our sins, and to cleanse us from all unrighteousness" (1 John 1:9).

**Cleansing:** "Your guilt is taken away, and your sin atoned for."

This is an act of purification. Purification is the removing of impurities from something or someone to restore the person to a state of newness. The Holy Spirit gives newness to our lives. We acquire new ways of thinking. We have new affections. We have new energy and fresh zeal for mission. Indeed, old things are passed away, and all things have become new. We are ready to testify that "my eyes have seen."

**Sending:** "Here I am, send me."

God makes us ready for the mission. He reveals His glory to us. He leads us to repentance and confession. He gives us a new life. He then challenges us to response to His goodness. He says, 'I make Myself available to you; will you now make yourself available to Me?' He asks "Who will go?" God made Isaiah ready, and he went. God made Paul ready, and he went. God made Moses ready, and he went. Has God prepared you through the process of conversion?

# The Structure of the Program—Conducting A Prayer Conference In Your Local Church

## Pre-Prayer Conference
**Planning**
Work with your team and plan the details of the program.

Friday, Sabbath, and Sunday

Choose your speaker(s) carefully and prayerfully.

Consult with your keynote speaker(s) to verify the following: texts, songs, needs (electronic and other visuals)

Budget for the program

**Resources**
Speakers' honorarium

Speakers' accommodations if they are coming from out of town

Food, if you are eating together as a church.

Other material that you may include: paper, writing material, prayer box, basket, candles (if you plan to use them).

**Personal Preparation**
A prayer conference is a time of refreshing and renewal with God. Therefore, it is important to prepare your heart and the hearts of the church members as well. Spend extra time with God in prayer during the weeks leading up to the conference. Ask God for guidance, cleansing, and pardon from all sins. Go to individuals who may be unhappy with you and ask forgiveness and provide forgiveness. Ensure that your heart is in the right place and there is nothing between you and your Savior. Thank God in advance for what He will do for you during this week. Get ready for the outpouring of the Spirit and the transformation that will come as a result of this weekend.

**Physical preparation**
Get the physical church ready for the weekend. Prepare the prayer box/prayer basket and altar building material. Prepare the prayer room (choose your color scheme—some people like white, purple, blue, or gold); secure white tablecloths and coverings/ribbons to match your color scheme; secure area rugs or cushions for kneeling, pre-recorded soothing music, paper and writing material, white chair covers, freshly cut floral arrangements, and green plants.

Have soothing pre-recorded music for the main sanctuary. Organize the prayer team, deacons, deaconesses, praise team, and other leaders to ensure that the program operates smoothly. Invite visitors who are not Adventist to attend.

A prayer conference is a revival. Therefore, plan and prepare for baptisms to take place. Prepare the baptismal pool, robes, and certificates. Identify people who attend church regularly and are not yet baptized members, invite your relatives and friends, and begin working with your children who have not yet given their hearts over to God in baptism.

# Friday Evening

| | |
|---|---|
| Setting the pace | Special music |
| Readiness in spiritual presence | Scriptural meditation |
| Music—soft, calming, spirit-filled | Bible reading |
| Hymnal music | Prayer and praise |

Scriptural meditation and response in prayer

Prayer points

PowerPoint or no PowerPoint
It may be better to allow the people to read the Bible and get into the Word. The PowerPoint may distract from truly meditating on God's Word

## The Sabbath Morning Program

Recorded music

Meditation

Music

Bible reading

Presentation 1

Prayer format

Singing

Prayer response

Presentation 2

Prayer format

Singing

Prayer response

Presentation 3

Prayer format

Singing

Meditation

Prayer response

## Sabbath Afternoon

Prayer walk

Singing

Meditation

Testimonies after the prayer walk

## Sunday Morning

Prayer

Singing

Reading the word

Prayer

Responding to God in writing, discussion in pairs, sharing

Presentation on "The Healing Power of Forgiveness"

Response

Singing

Anointing

Testimonies

Prayer breakfast

Organize the hospitality team to prepare a breakfast consisting of fruits, salads, and other menu items that you deem appropriate.

# *References*

Dybdahl, J. (Ed.). (2010). *Andrews Study Bible: Light. Depth. Truth.* Berrien Springs, MI: Andrews University Press.

Nilson, B. L. (2010). *Teaching at Its Best: A Research-Based Resource for College Instructors*. San Francisco, CA: Jossey-Bass.

Wahlen, C. (2014). *The Book of James Adult Sabbath School Quarterly 4Q 2014*. Nampa, ID: Pacific Press.

White, E. G. (2002). *Prayer*. Nampa, ID: Pacific Press.

Wilkinson, Bruce. (2002). *A life God rewards*. Sisters, OR: Multnomah.

Wilkinson, Bruce. (2001). *Secrets of the Vine*. Sisters, OR: Multnomah.

*Women of Destiny Bible. Women Mentoring Women Through the Scriptures.* (2000). Nashville, TN: Thomas Nelson.

## TEACH Services, Inc.
PUBLISHING

We invite you to view the complete
selection of titles we publish at:
**www.TEACHServices.com**

We encourage you to write us
with your thoughts about this,
or any other book we publish at:
**info@TEACHServices.com**

TEACH Services' titles may be purchased in
bulk quantities for educational, fund-raising,
business, or promotional use.
**bulksales@TEACHServices.com**

Finally, if you are interested in seeing
your own book in print, please contact us at:
**publishing@TEACHServices.com**

We are happy to review your manuscript at no charge.